First Encounters

FIRST ENCOUNTERS

A Book of Memorable Meetings

by

Nancy Caldwell Sorel

and Edward Sorel

Alfred A. Knopf New York 1996

THIS IS A BORZOI BOOK
PUBLISHED BY ALFRED A. KNOPF, INC.

All of the material in this work was originally published in *The Atlantic Monthly*.

Library of Congress Cataloging-in-Publication Data
Sorel, Nancy Caldwell, [date]
First encounters : a book of memorable meetings / by Nancy Caldwell Sorel and
Edward Sorel. — 1st ed.
p. cm.
ISBN 0-679-43119-5
1. Celebrities—Caricatures and cartoons. 2. American wit and humor, Pictorial.
3. Celebrities—Anecdotes. I. Sorel, Edward. II. Title.
NC1429.S568A4 1994
741.5´973—dc20   93-21026   CIP

Manufactured in Italy
Published October 13, 1994
Second Printing, July 1996

For
Madeline,
Leo,
Jenny,
and
Katherine

Contents

Acknowledgments

We are first of all deeply indebted to William Whitworth, editor of *The Atlantic Monthly*, who twelve years ago took a chance on an offbeat idea called "First Encounters," and has supported us in it ever since. Cullen Murphy, managing editor and a fine writer himself, has provided the ever-watchful care under which contributors thrive. Judy Garlan, art director, and Sue Parilla, associate editor, have also been invaluable.

We are especially grateful to our agent, Irene Skolnick; our editor, Ann Close; and our loyal friends at Knopf, Katherine Hourigan, Anthea Lingeman, and Nina Bourne. Our warm appreciation also goes to Marcus Ratliff for his design direction. Thanks as well to all those readers—many of whom we have never met—who when they came across a delicious first encounter in their reading, thought of us and sent it along.

Without the superb resources of the New York Public Library Research Collection and Picture Collection, this endeavor would have foundered long ago. Finally, we wish to acknowledge the inspiration provided by the fictional "Impossible Interviews" Miguel Covarrubias illustrated for *Vanity Fair* in the 1920s and '30s. They made us wonder how much more interesting actual first meetings might be.

First Encounters

Frédéric Chopin
George Sand

LIKE ONE OF HIS OWN PRELUDES, Chopin's first encounter with George Sand arrived at its logical conclusion with no promise of there ever being more to come. It took place in Paris in the fall of 1836. Franz Liszt, intimate friend of both, had long wished them to meet, but Chopin had resisted. He abhorred intellectualizing in general, by women in particular. His tastes were as delicate as his constitution. He liked his women young, beautiful, of impeccable ancestry, preferably innocent, at the very least discreet. George Sand was none of the above.

An introduction became inevitable, however, when Sand moved into rooms below those shared by Liszt and his mistress, Countess Marie d'Agoult, at the Hôtel de France, not far from Chopin's apartment at 38, rue de la Chaussée d'Antin. Madame Sand had therefore to be included in the small soirée at Chopin's on November 5. Franz, Marie, and George arrived together. Chopin, fragile and charming, with his aquiline nose, long tapering fingers, and aristo-cratic manner, found himself greeting a small (less than five feet tall) dark-haired woman clearly older (by six years) than he who wore—as he had been warned to expect—pants.

It was an exceptionally relaxed evening. Chopin clowned about gently with his guests, trying not to be appalled by Sand, who puffed away at her cigar, philosophized madly, and addressed all alike in the second person singular. Tea was served. Later both Chopin and Liszt played. The latter exuded his usual virile charm, but in deference to the assembled company Sand did not take her accustomed position, crouched in an ecstatic ball under the piano. She became, instead, especially when Chopin performed, cool and aloof, the detached observer. It was a role played for his benefit, but Chopin did not know that yet. "I have made the acquaintance of a great celebrity: Madame Dudevant, known by the name of George Sand," he wrote home to his family in Poland. "Her appearance is not to my liking and doesn't please me at all."

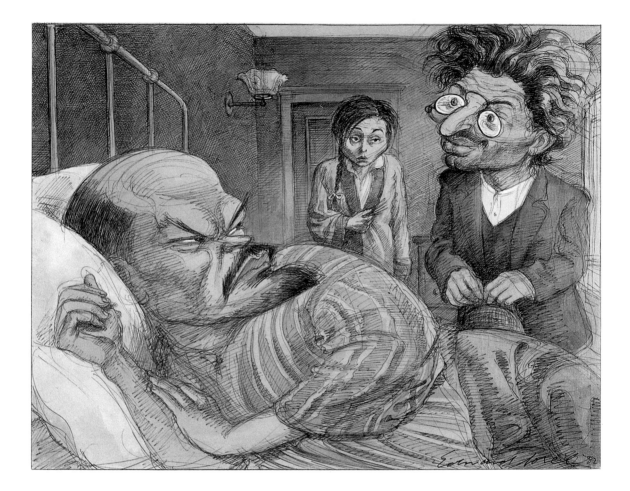

Lenin
Trotsky

VLADIMIR ILYICH ULYANOV, alias Lenin, was still asleep when Lev Davidovich Bronstein, alias Trotsky, plunked himself down on his doorstep.

It was October 1902; the place, London; the hour, dawn. Both men were in exile; both were alumni of the czar's prisons in and out of Siberia; both had escaped; both were totally immersed in and dedicated to the Marxist revolutionary movement, of which Lenin, at thirty-two, was the acknowledged head. His current command post was London. A number of his compatriot revolutionaries had congregated there, crowded into communes; Lenin, however, lived apart. So many people, he said, affected his nerves. He and his wife, Krupskaya, occupied a flat in one of the seedier neighborhoods (not far from the shabby rooms where, nearly a half-century before—surrounded by wife, mistress-servant, brood of children, and horde of creditors—the apparently nerveless Karl Marx had produced *Das Kapital*).

Trotsky was twenty-two years old. Papa Bronstein, a barely literate Russian Jewish farmer, had educated him to become an engineer; my son the revolutionary was not what he had in mind. Nor had he expected the sojourns in the prisons of Odessa, the marriage to a Gentile woman ten years his senior, the two children born in the Siberian tundra. From Siberia, Trotsky wrote in secret the fiery tracts on Marxist theory that found their way to London, earning him the sobriquet "the Pen" and a summons from Lenin.

Trotsky arrived penniless. Despite the hour, he took a cab to the address jotted down on a scrap of paper. Krupskaya answered the prescribed triple knock in her nightclothes, which Trotsky hardly noticed, concerned only that she address him in Russian (he spoke no English) and pay for the taxi. Krupskaya explained that Lenin was still asleep. He had trouble falling asleep nights, she said; he would lie in bed for hours reading French grammars to calm his nerves. But Trotsky was expected. She ushered him unceremoniously into the bedroom. "Vladimir Ilyich," she said, "the Pen has arrived."

Greta Garbo

John Barrymore

He SHOWED UP AT THE STUDIO early, and sober, an indication that he regarded *Grand Hotel* with less than his usual cynicism. Barrymore—a name synonymous with dashing grace and romance—was just turning fifty that January of 1932, and the role of the Baron von Geigern, a nobleman on the skids, was one he understood. He was less comfortable with the idea that Grusinskaya would be played by the beautiful but inscrutable Greta Garbo, aged twenty-six. Barrymore had never met Garbo. Garbo, by choice, never met anyone.

Hence his discomposure as he waited that morning. For the first time in his long career, he had drawn a leading lady whose following was greater than his own. She also made more money. She was reputed to be aloof, diffident, antisocial. The script called for them to fall in love at first sight, but how, damn it, did one make love—even screen love—to a misanthrope? Along with all that, she was apparently temperamental—nine o'clock had come and gone, and where was she?

She was, as he soon discovered, outside the entrance, where she had been waiting for him to arrive. She wished to "honor the great Barrymore" by personally escorting him onto the set. He was touched, perhaps rumors were exaggerated. He met her halfway, raised her hand to his lips, looked into her eyes. The Baron von Barrymore, ageless, took over.

As filming proceeded, so did the relationship. "You are the most entrancing woman in the world," he would whisper when he sensed she felt insecure. She, in turn, was almost maternal—doctored his hangovers with her own concoction, and spent an entire lunch break rearranging a couch so that in the forthcoming love scene his celebrated left profile would be toward the camera.

Grand Hotel was their only movie together. Asked about her years later, Barrymore, usually the raconteur, elected to out-Garbo Garbo. "She is a fine lady and a great actress," he said, and paused. "And the rest is silence."

Gustav Mahler

Sigmund Freud

THEY WERE JEWS by birth (unreligious, but puritanical) and Viennese by adoption. Freud had been a medical student in Vienna when Mahler was at the conservatory. Later Mahler served as conductor of the Vienna Court Opera. Opera was one of Freud's few diversions. But they did not meet until Freud was fifty-four and Mahler, at fifty, had less than a year to live.

The encounter was occasioned by the composer's marital problems with the young and beautiful Alma. Engrossed in his Tenth Symphony, Mahler suddenly found himself the object of domestic rebellion. Alma had, she said, submitted to his tyranny and neglect long enough; she felt used, drained by his self-absorption. The truth of her accusations, together with a case of impotence, produced in Mahler both guilt and panic—panic that was not eased by the appearance of another man (Walter Gropius) on the scene. Immediate action was called for.

Freud, vacationing in Leyden, Holland, that summer of 1910, received a telegram asking for an appointment. The following day came another telegram, canceling. Mahler's vacillation was repeated twice more before he managed to conquer his resistance. He and Freud met in a Leyden hotel and spent the next four hours strolling about the town—the stocky, confident doctor and the thin, intense composer—smoking the cigars both adored. Freud conducted a sort of mini-analysis. A mother fixation was diagnosed: Mahler was attracted by his wife's youthful beauty but resented that she was not old and careworn like his mother. Alma, to even things out, had a father complex and found her husband's age appealing. Mahler was reassured.

The two men parted friends. Mahler's potency returned, and psychoanalysis got the credit. Alma said later that Freud had reproached her husband for marrying one so young, but his attitude was closer to sympathy than to censure. A good wife—in Freud's view as in Mahler's—was but a ministering angel put on earth for the comfort and support of her husband.

James Joyce
T. S. Eliot

THEY MET AT THE Hôtel de l'Elysée, in Paris, on August 15, 1920. Joyce, who had gone about that summer in dirty tennis shoes, to much comment, put on black patents for the occasion, and took his fifteen-year-old son, Giorgio, along. Eliot—tall, handsome, sartorially irreproachable—came over from London with Wyndham Lewis. After introductions, they sat around a small table on which lay a crumpled, intricately knotted brown parcel sent to Joyce through Eliot by their mutual friend Ezra Pound. Pound's motive was double-edged. A kind of literary missionary, he was sure that Eliot and Joyce had more in common than the fact that both were expatriates, had worked (Eliot still did) as bank clerks, were chronically short of funds.

Hence the package. The author of "Prufrock" waved a hand in its direction; he was unburdened, his mission accomplished. The author of *Portrait* was less pleased. Straw boater in hand, patents prominent, Joyce was clearly reluctant to claim anything so untidy. Besides, it was hopelessly knotted, and no one had a penknife. Nail scissors were produced. Finally the layers of swaddling were unwound to reveal . . . a pair of old brown shoes.

It was Eliot—tactful, Boston-mannered Eliot—who suggested dinner. Joyce would join them, would he not? He would. Joyce perceived but one way to regain his Irish dignity. Giorgio was packed off with the unhappy parcel, and Joyce conducted his new friends to his favorite restaurant, where he selected the table, ordered an excellent dinner with wines, and picked up the tab.

Joyce repeated this hospitality several times during Eliot's stay. Their friendship remained cool, but two years later, when *The Waste Land* and *Ulysses* fell in a single burst upon the literary establishment, a rather grudging kinship emerged. Eliot looked to Joyce for support when he separated from his wife. Joyce, for his part, tried his hand at parodying *The Waste Land* with lines that began, "Rouen is the rainiest place getting / Inside all impermeables," and that concluded, significantly, "Hurry up, Joyce, it's time!"

Constantine Stanislavsky
Isadora Duncan

H<small>E WAS A WEALTHY</small> Russian aristocrat; she, an American of no name, dubious respectability, and erratic financial solvency. He spoke no English; she knew little Russian. She was fond of saying that she had learned to walk and to dance simultaneously, while he recalled incidents of monumental clumsiness from childhood. But art transcends, and both spoke French. "We understood each other," he said, "almost before we had said a single word."

In 1907, Isadora was in Moscow on her second crusade to confront the Russian public with what she regarded as an overdue alternative to classical ballet. By chance, Stanislavsky dropped in on a performance. In her customary dishabille, Isadora had executed several numbers before he sufficiently overcame the shock of "an almost naked body on the stage" to appraise her style. It was vibrant, arresting. When the first-act curtain brought rather tepid applause and scattered hissing, Stanislavsky strode indignantly to the edge of the stage, applauding defiantly. He was a large, impressive man, immediately recognizable as an actor and codirector of the Moscow Art Theater. The hissing stopped.

From then on, Stanislavsky attended all of Isadora's performances. He recognized in her dancing that "truth of the inner creative urge" he sought in acting. The artless unrestraint he strove for apparently was hers by nature. That same unrestraint, he soon found, extended to her offstage life. She was young, captivating; she invited him into her hotel room, and from there into her bed. But Stanislavsky was in his forties, long married to a prominent actress, and—like many Russians—puritanical. "But what should we do with a child?" "What child?" asked Isadora. "Why, our child, of course . . . I would never approve of any child of mine being raised outside my jurisdiction."

Years later, during her sojourn in post-revolutionary Russia, Isadora related the scene to Madame Stanislavsky. "Oh, but this is just like him," said the actress. "He takes life so seriously."

Frederick the Great
Voltaire

THEY CORRESPONDED prodigiously and effusively for four years. One wrote to "my Apollo," "my Socrates," the other to "my Trajan"; they enclosed their latest poems and swapped compliments accordingly. At last, in September 1740, the French playwright/poet/*philosophe* François-Marie Arouet, adopted name Voltaire, aged forty-five, was to meet Frederick, newly crowned king of Prussia, twenty-eight. Plans were laid; expectancy soared. "I am sure to faint from joy," wrote Voltaire. Responded Frederick, "I believe I shall die from it."

The meeting would appear doomed to anticlimax, but, on the contrary, Frederick staged it well, and Voltaire was a practiced actor.

Traveling incognito westward, Frederick fell ill with the four-day ague. He sent word shifting the rendezvous site to Moyland Castle, near Cleves (thereby avoiding Voltaire's mistress, the Marquise du Châtelet) and urging Voltaire to take a fast coach the 150 miles there. At Moyland, Voltaire found the king wrapped in a coarse blue dressing gown, lying on a narrow bed in a room sparsely furnished. Voltaire gave a courtly bow, Frederick a royal shiver. Superbly solicitous, Voltaire took the king's pulse, which so revived Frederick that he was able to get up, dress, dine, and discourse at majestic length on free will and the immortality of the soul.

After three days, they parted. Voltaire, persecuted in France, twice took up residence at the Prussian court. His second sojourn lasted more than two years, and the relationship barely survived. Frederick still wrote poetry, but had no qualms about plunging Europe into war.

In time the philosopher king was found to have a despotic bent. Voltaire concluded that the best of all possible worlds was seriously flawed; besides, there were no women at court. He engaged in a shady financial transaction, spied a bit on the side, poked fun at the king's poems, drank too much chocolate. His departure was maneuvered without either man's losing face, but the two were careful never to meet again.

Captain John Smith
Pocahontas

THEIR MEETING was the stuff of fairy tales. He was brave, clever, handsome (though a bit short), and had come from faraway lands. If he lacked the innocence of the archetypal prince, and she the fair complexion decreed for a princess, these were minor aberrations. The script was right. He was being held captive by her father, the powerful chief-king; she alone could rescue him from certain death. Later on, although she was barely thirteen, they would marry and live happily ever after. Pocahontas, being a real princess, understood her role. Captain John Smith, a commoner, bungled his.

In the winter of 1607–1608, Smith, out foraging for the hungry settlers at Jamestown, was captured and taken to Werowocomoco to face Powhatan. Some two hundred Algonkians crowded into the longhouse. Words were spoken; pipes smoked. Then, as Smith wrote later, "two great stones were brought," and right on cue came the piercing cry and running feet, the young body thrown over his, bare arms cradling his head. Pocahontas, his savior.

His savior—unless, of course, it was all an act. Unless it was merely a traditional tribal sacrament of the execution-rescue variety, not uncommon among the Algonkians. The lives of chiefs were as a rule spared, and Smith was viewed (erroneously) as the White Chief. The Dark Princess saves the White Chief—standard ritual melodrama. Only Smith misunderstood.

Or, perhaps, pretended to misunderstand. His account alone survives. Ambitious for advancement back in England, he knew the charge of miscegenation could be disastrous. For two long winters an adoring Pocahontas brought the captain food for his starving band. Then, in 1609, he sailed to England without so much as a good-bye. Abandoned his princess. Ignored his clear obligation. Left her to mourn, to grieve, to resort finally to the dependable, if pedestrian, John Rolfe.

Smith never did marry—give him that. He never realized success, either. And he turned the whole fairy tale askew.

Fats Waller

Al Capone

P ROHIBITION REIGNED that New Year of 1926, and Chicago was a wide-open town. When the mobs staked out their territories, he who trespassed died—rubbed out by hired hands. Alphonse "Al" Capone had made his share of "arrangements." Recent mass carnage had left him sole proprietor of a chain of breweries, brothels, speakeasies, and gambling dens that netted millions. The press, politicians, and the police were all in his pocket. He was twenty-seven.

Thomas "Fats" Waller was another kind of prodigy. To him, a "mob" was what packed in to hear you at Harlem rent parties. The "family" were your musical mentors, people like James P. Johnson and Willie "the Lion" Smith; an "arrangement" was something you did on the piano. His experience with booze and women was strictly from the consumption end, and his only brush with the law was dodging the process server to avoid paying alimony. When Fats left New York for Chicago to play a few gigs, he was twenty-one years old.

The ebullient young man with the dazzling jazz style was a big hit at the Sherman Hotel. His nightly audience included men with wide lapels and bulging pockets. One evening Fats felt a revolver poked into his paunchy stomach. He found himself bullied into a black limousine, heard the driver ordered to East Cicero. Sweat pouring down his body, Fats foresaw a premature end to his career, but on arrival at a fancy saloon, he was merely pushed toward a piano and told to play. He played. Loudest in applause was a beefy man with an unmistakable scar: Al Capone was having a birthday, and he, Fats, was a present from "the boys."

The party lasted three days. Fats exhausted himself and his repertoire, but with every request bills were stuffed into his pockets. He and Capone consumed vast quantities of food and drink. By the time the black limousine headed back to the Sherman, Fats had acquired several thousand dollars in cash and a decided taste for vintage champagne.

Charlie Chaplin
Jean Cocteau

CHARLIE CHAPLIN'S first encounter with Jean Cocteau was memorable not so much for its improbability (on a Japanese boat in the South China Sea) or its spirit (friendly enough) as for the marked disinclination it inspired in either man for any second encounter.

It was 1936. *Modern Times* had just been released, and its creator had taken its leading lady—his wife, Paulette Goddard—on an extended trip to the Orient. Embarking at Singapore, he was handed a note from Cocteau, whose recent film *Le Sang d'un poète* was a critical success, and who was there doing a story for *Le Figaro*. Would M. Chaplin, the note read, join him in his cabin for an aperitif before dinner?

M. Chaplin was delighted, although less so on discovering that just as he spoke no French, Cocteau spoke no English. Communication was carried on through the deadpan translations of Cocteau's secretary: "Meester Cocteau . . . he say . . . you are a poet . . . of ze sunshine . . . and he is a poet of ze . . . night." Still, their shared enthusiasms were enough to carry them along until four in the morning, and they promised to meet for lunch.

With the bright light of noon, however, came cold reality. They had said all they had to say to each other. Both men passed up lunch and spent the afternoon composing notes of apology, which crossed. Desperation set in.

But the dilemma was a shared one. Circumvention became the game of the day. It was understood that Cocteau lunched with his secretary, and Chaplin dined with Paulette. If during the morning promenade they should catch a glimpse of each other, the one closer to a door would promptly duck inside. Both grew familiar with parts of the boat they had not known existed. Gradually, they relaxed. By the time Tokyo was reached, salutations—even brief conversation—were possible.

The ironies became apparent only later. Paulette, who saw a great deal of Chaplin on that trip, was estranged from him within the year, but Cocteau remained a faithful, if distant, friend forever.

Enrico Caruso
Giacomo Puccini

THE PLOT WAS NOT so much Italian opera as Hollywood musical. A young man and woman are in love. She is to star in a show; he wishes to play opposite her, but he is unknown. She challenges him to audition before the composer himself; he accepts, overrides all obstacles of protocol, and performs with such stunning artistry and style that the role is instantly his.

A promising stratagem, but our lover did not look the part. He was short and tubby, with an undistinguished moustache and an undesirable Neapolitan accent. It was the composer who was handsome and debonair. What our lover did have was the optimism of youth: with all the engaging audacity of a movie hero, Enrico Caruso, desirous of singing Rodolfo in *La Bohème*, arrived unannounced one day in June 1897, in the Tuscan village of Torre del Lago, at the house of Giacomo Puccini.

He was admitted under protest. Puccini, ultrasensitive to cold, a wide-brimmed hat on his head, ushered him into a studio made stifling by a roaring fire. Perspiring from heat and nervousness, Caruso asked to sing "Che gelida manina." Puccini obligingly sat down at the piano. It took only a few bars for the composer to realize that in tone and dramatic intensity here was the perfect—the ultimate—Rodolfo. With the final high C, Puccini spun around in genuine amazement. "Who has sent you to me?" he asked. "God?"

Caruso sang Rodolfo opposite his mistress (who would bear him two sons and then leave him for the chauffeur). He later triumphed in *Tosca* and *Madama Butterfly*. As the careers of both men rose to meteoric heights, they became warm, if sometimes wary, friends. It irked Puccini that Caruso was getting rich ($100,000 a year) recording his (Puccini's) arias through that bell-shaped tin horn, to be sold on those scratchy waxed discs, for which he himself as yet got nothing. He wrote to a friend that Caruso was "lazy" and "too pleased with himself." "All the same," Puccini could not help but add, "his voice is magnificent."

Sarah Bernhardt

Thomas Alva Edison

AFTERWARD SHE CLAIMED that he was "intensely bored" by the prospect of her visit. Not likely. She was, after all, the incomparable Sarah, on her first tour of America, and Edison, who had been stagestruck in his youth and who cherished a secret image of himself as a tragedian, might have been apprehensive, but not bored. Besides, her visit provided excellent publicity for his new incandescent lamp.

Her motives are less clear. She had finished her New York run and was en route to Boston; Menlo Park, New Jersey, lay in the opposite direction. What in that cold, snowy December of 1880 prompted so deliberate a detour? Perhaps the same sense of adventure that impelled her to ride out onto the partially built Brooklyn Bridge, to go down into a Pennsylvania coal mine, and to leap about on the ice floes of the St. Lawrence. Was not the thirty-three-year-old inventor another American wonder to be experienced?

The train reached Menlo Park at two a.m.—little problem for the routinely nocturnal Edison; more of one for Mrs. E., who had prepared supper. Dimly lit carriages transported Bernhardt's party along the dark road. As they neared the house, she saw "the whole country suddenly illuminated." Hundreds of electric lights strung from the trees were reflected by the snow to dazzling effect. The carriage stopped; she alighted. Edison took her extended hand.

Later, touring the lab, the sylphid actress followed her host up and down ladder-like stairways, admiring the machinery, applauding the flashing lights, nodding in response to his running commentary in a language she did not understand. She spoke some lines from *Phèdre* into the marvelous phonograph. She must have it! He would have one specially made. She took his arm; in this short time they were the best of friends. He bore, she decided, a striking resemblance to Napoleon. Gazing over a balustrade into an abyss of revolving wheels and belts, she paid him her ultimate dramatic compliment—she fainted away in his arms.

Felix Mendelssohn

Victoria R.

ONE HAD TO BE CAREFUL, Victoria and Albert agreed, about foreign musicians. Many of them drank and were involved with women. But this Mendelssohn was a gentleman and family man, always invited to the best houses when he came to England. At thirty-three he was only ten years older than they were. They often sang duets from one of his song collections and had heard that he played superbly; his Jewish ancestry seemed hardly to matter—really, not at all. When he played the organ at St. Paul's, all London went to listen. Albert played the organ, too. Music was, Victoria said—after herself and the children, of course—his greatest love.

So Felix was invited to Buckingham Palace, after dinner, one June evening in 1842. Victoria and Albert were almost fluttery with anticipation. They accompanied the composer to the piano and listened with rapt attention as he played selections from his *Songs Without Words*. When he asked them for a theme to improvise on, they enthusiastically offered two, and the queen much admired his rendition of the Austrian national anthem with the right hand and "Rule, Britannia" with the left. "Really I have never heard anything so beautiful," she wrote in her diary, adding, "Poor Mendelssohn was quite exhausted when he had done playing."

Needless to say, he was asked back. Albert wanted Felix to try his organ, and Victoria wanted what Albert wanted, so there was Mendelssohn, on a Saturday afternoon, at Buckingham again. The prince explained the organ registers and played a chorale. Felix followed with the chorus from *St. Paul*, the three of them singing along and Albert pulling the stops. Next they trooped to the queen's salon, where, at the piano, Victoria sang "Italien." Except that she sang D sharp where it should have been natural, as Mendelssohn later reported, and natural where it should have been sharp, she performed "most charmingly." In fact, he said, "the only really nice, comfortable house in England, one where one feels completely at home, is Buckingham Palace."

William Randolph Hearst
Orson Welles

ORSON WELLES always denied that *Citizen Kane* was the story of William Randolph Hearst, but of course, it was. The parallels are obvious. Both Hearst and Charles Foster Kane were born in 1863, were symbiotically attached to their mothers, were kicked out of Harvard, and went on to amass newspaper empires. Both ran for political office and lost, although Hearst ran and lost more often (including a bid for the Democratic presidential ticket in 1904). Xanadu was a carbon copy of San Simeon, and Susan—with her blond hair, artistic aspirations, and addiction to jigsaw puzzles—a caricature of Marion Davies. Hearst was not amused.

No time was lost mobilizing forces against Welles and RKO. The studio, harassed by the Hearst press—thirty of the most influential papers in the country—found its position vulnerable. A word in the ear of Nelson Rockefeller, and Radio City Music Hall became unavailable; the same thing happened at theaters all over the country. Financial disaster loomed. Hollywood itself was hostile: at twenty-five Welles was already a daring and successful director/producer/star both on stage and in radio, and was far from humble about it. His arrogance made it easy for Louella Parsons to attack the man who attacked her boss. Louis B. Mayer, Hearst's old buddy (MGM produced many Marion Davies films), offered to buy the negative and prints of *Citizen Kane* and destroy them, but RKO finally permitted the film's release, on May 1, 1941.

By chance the old lion and the cocky cub crossed paths not long afterward. On the day of the San Francisco opening (as Welles told the story later), the two adversaries found themselves alone together in the elevator of the Fairmont Hotel. Welles could not ignore such potential for drama. Oozing charm, he introduced himself as the son of the publisher's old friend Richard Welles and invited Hearst to the premiere. His overture was met with stony silence. As Hearst got off at his floor, Welles, rebuffed but unrelenting, delivered his final shot: "Charles Foster Kane would have *accepted*."

Dorothy Parker
Dashiell Hammett

D ASHIELL HAMMETT was clearly off his guard. Sam Spade would have cased the joint on arrival, spotted the phonies and deadbeats, reconnoitered. But Hammett, old Pinkerton sleuth that he was, had grown soft and careless in sunny, moneyed Hollywood. Escorting his friend Lillian Hellman to a New York cocktail party in the fall of 1931, he shrugged off precaution, and paid for it.

He had scarcely accepted his first drink when he was introduced to a tiny, dark-eyed woman who, without warning, dropped dramatically to her silk-stockinged knees, grasped his hand, and kissed it. Stunned, Hammett stared icily down at her. Of course he knew of Dorothy Parker, reigning lady of the Algonquin luncheon set, author of quirky little poems and sad little stories. More to the point, she had in a recent review called him a "hell-bent, cold-hearted writer" and meant it as praise. But public displays of adulation were less welcome. Hammett hated flamboyance; women should be self-possessed, controlled. Miss Wonderly never lost her cool.

It was a bad beginning, and although Hammett and Parker were closely associated for the rest of their lives, the relationship never much improved. As screenwriters in Hollywood in the 1930s, both enjoyed fat salaries for little work accomplished, and both spent the money frivolously, madly, as if ashamed to have it. Both drank too much, often in the same company, and they served together on committees for such causes as aiding Loyalist Spain, unionizing film writers, and combating anti-Semitism. Hammett admired her wit and her investigative talent for ferreting information out of people without their realizing it, but not her predilection for turning that information humorously yet treacherously against them. He could not reconcile her contradictions. Hellman, intimate friend of both, would try to intercede, but it was quite literally a case of Dash/Dot, Dot/Dash, opposing entities, and invariably when Parker came to visit, Hammett moved elsewhere for the duration. Sam Spade never went looking for trouble.

Igor Stravinsky
W. H. Auden

WHEN STRAVINSKY INVITED Auden to come to Hollywood (from New York) in November 1947, to work on the projected opera *The Rake's Progress*, Auden was, by his own admission, scared stiff. He had greatly admired the composer ever since, at age sixteen, he had bought *Three Easy Pieces*. But a week was a long time. Stravinsky might well turn out to be a tempestuous Russian prima donna. Should he, Auden, pack a dinner jacket? Kiss hands on arrival *à la russe?*

On the other coast, Igor and Vera were experiencing similar qualms. Modern English poetry was not within the composer's expertise, but he had been assured (by his neighbor Aldous Huxley) that Wystan was the best and would produce a superb libretto. The question thus became not how good he was but how tall. Would he or would he not fit on the couch in the den?

Auden arrived, and it was immediately apparent that he would not, but it was apparent also that it wouldn't matter. He consumed an enormous dinner and gulped down quantities of wine. Exactly at ten-thirty he was ready for bed. The fatherly Stravinsky, who had sons about Auden's age, brought a chair and pillows to extend the couch, and Auden retired. At eight he was up and ready—after a little coffee topped with whisky—for the day's work.

In fact, the two brilliant innovators—each with a strong work ethic—got along quite well. If the proper, dapper little composer was taken aback by his guest's careless attire and the maid's report that the soap and towels in his bath were never touched, and if the poet, accustomed to a solitary cat, was unprepared for forty garrulous parrots and lovebirds, the two nevertheless delighted in each other's company. *The Rake* progressed. The scenario completed, Auden returned to New York, but correspondence flourished. Acts 1 and 2 flew westward, and by the time they met again, the following March, the composer was smothering the poet with Russian bear hugs, and Auden was referring to him and Vera affectionately as "the Stravs."

Fritz Lang

Dr. Joseph Goebbels

I T WAS SPRING 1933, in Berlin, and Hitler was only briefly in the chancellery. Fritz Lang, in striped trousers and morning coat, arrived at the palace on the Wilhelmplatz, now the Ministry for National Enlightenment and Propaganda. Brown-shirted storm troopers were conspicuous, and by the time he was ushered into the large, high-windowed office, Lang was sweating profusely. Facing him was a little man in the uniform (custommade) of the National Socialist Party. Lang, the celebrated movie director of the Weimar Republic, had been summoned by Dr. Joseph Goebbels of the Third Reich.

The interview, Lang assumed, was to chastise him for putting Nazi slogans into the mouth of a psychopath in his newly completed film, *The Last Will of Dr. Mabuse*. But the Herr Doktor was all charm and condescension. A movie fanatic, he saw all Lang's films, although he might, as he did with *Mabuse*, ban them afterward. He had sent for Lang because Hitler admired *Metropolis* and wanted Lang as a sort of Reichsminister of film.

Lang was alarmed. Recently Goebbels had spoken to producers about the need to "reestablish film on a healthy basis," meaning an Aryan one. Lang mentioned his Jewish ancestry on his mother's side. Goebbels noted that such a drawback might be overlooked. He chatted on while Lang, who had no intention of accepting the post, worried that the bank would close before he could get his money out. (It did.) Released at last, and having promised Goebbels an answer within twenty-four hours, Lang returned home, collected 500 marks and some jewelry, and boarded the night train for Paris. He slit the carpeting of his compartment to hide the money and taped the jewelry to the pipes in the lavatory, then retrieved everything once he had crossed the border.

Over the next decade Goebbels developed propaganda into a high art and oversaw nearly every film made in the Reich. Lang, in America, discovered that he had only exchanged Nazi tyranny for that of the Hollywood producer, but it was a trade-off he never regretted.

F. Scott Fitzgerald

Edith Wharton

TO YOUR GENERATION," Edith Wharton wrote from her estate outside Paris to Scott Fitzgerald at his flat near the place de l'Etoile, ". . . I must represent the literary equivalent of tufted furniture and gas chandeliers."

If true, it was only half the story. To Fitzgerald she embodied an enviable conjunction of wealth and social connection, prodigious authorship, critical success, and intimate association with the artistic upper crust. It was a persona he much admired. According to him, two years previously, when she had been in New York at Scribners, their common publisher, he had barged into the office and knelt in obeisance at her feet. If such a meeting took place, she made no mention of it when, in that summer of 1925, she wrote to thank Scott for sending *The Great Gatsby*, just out, and to invite him and Zelda to tea.

Zelda refused. She would not go and be made to "feel provincial," so Fitzgerald took along Teddy Chanler, a Wharton family friend. As to what occurred, we have Scott's version, Teddy's version, Teddy's revised version, and Zelda's version of Scott's version. First Scott warded off his apprehensions with a few (many) drinks on the drive out. The tea party in the elegantly furnished sitting room was rather formal (boring), and to enliven it Scott rose, strolled (weaved) (staggered) across to the fireplace, leaned picturesquely (tipsily) against the mantel, and began a story about a naive American couple who spent three days (two weeks) in a Paris bordello, thinking it was a hotel. End of story. His hostess, whom he had expected to register shock, expressed only irritation. Where was the plot, the detail? "But Mr. Fitzgerald," she said, refilling his cup, "you haven't told us what they *did* in the bordello."

Poor Scott. The visit proved a—well, sobering experience. He had thought to be audacious and had emerged merely jejune: he had failed his generation. We are left with Edith Wharton's version, summed up in her diary: "To tea, Teddy Chanler and Scott Fitzgerald, the novelist (awful)."

Fanny Brice

Florenz Ziegfeld

To Flo Ziegfeld, entrepreneur of the sensual, a comedian was someone who kept audiences distracted while his beloved chorus girls were changing costumes. Still, he would have the best—Will Rogers, W. C. Fields, Bert Williams—and when he heard Fanny sing "Sadie Salome, Go Home" with a Yiddish accent in a Broadway burlesque, he knew that with her onstage his girls could take their time.

Fanny Brice was almost nineteen. She had been born on the Lower East Side and brought up above a saloon in Newark. She was tall and skinny—a drawback in 1910, when chorus girls were at the very least statuesque. Skinny was funny. A comedian could capitalize on skinny.

The dream of every dancer, singer, and comic in America was to make the Follies, so on the day Fanny arrived at work and was handed a telegram signed "Florenz Ziegfeld," she thought it was a joke. Still, what if . . . She didn't know that correspondence by telegram was Ziegfeld's style. On a hunch she telephoned. A moment later she was whooping down Broadway.

But in Ziegfeld's presence she was suddenly speechless. She sat, knees together, fingers locked, hardly raising her eyes, and even when he offered her a job, she could answer only in monosyllables. Yes, she had been underage when she signed her present contract (thank God). No, her mother had not cosigned it: her mother could not read or write (*Gott sei dank*). Yes, seventy-five dollars a week, next year a hundred, *would* do.

After she signed the Follies contract, Fanny recovered enough to thank Ziegfeld in her most ladylike manner. She thanked the secretary. She thanked the doorman. Then she raced back down Broadway and stood outside the burlesque house all afternoon, grabbing people, *showing* them.

Many more contracts followed. For twenty years Fanny sang her funny/sad songs and lampooned ballet dancers in graceful poses and society ladies from Sutton Place and Oyster Bay. And Ziegfeld smiled his tender smile and wrote out his generous checks, because the Follies wasn't the Follies without Fanny.

Joseph Conrad
Lady Ottoline Morrell

TURNING FORTY that summer of 1913 put Lady Ottoline Morrell in mind of things yet to be done. She had still, for example, to meet Joseph Conrad and entice him to one of her Thursdays. She *did* admire him—would Henry James serve as intermediary? "But dear lady . . . but dear lady," James expostulated, pacing the length of her gray drawing room at Bedford Square. "He has lived his life at sea—dear lady, he has never met 'civilized' women." Conrad would not *understand* her, James said; as for Conrad's wife, she was a "good cook"—a dubious talent. But he provided the introduction.

Conrad responded warily. Lady Ottoline's Bloomsbury reputation as society hostess on the prowl had no doubt traveled even to the farther reaches of Kent. And her presence! "Like a Spanish galleon, hung with golden coins and lovely silken sails," wrote Virginia Woolf. Others termed it "overdone." There were rumors, too, of lovers—the painters Augustus John, Henry Lamb, maybe even Roger Fry, and that odd mathematician Bertrand Russell. Conrad replied that he was not, after all, very interesting, and declined her invitation.

No matter. Lady Ottoline would come down to Kent herself by train. (If she could not display him, she would at least describe him.) At his moated farmhouse, Conrad, conservatively attired in double-breasted blue, awaited her. His welcome was formal (she *was* half sister to a duke), but later he opened up and spoke of the past the Congo, the sea—and of his present difficulties with his writing. Most thrilling was when he touched on his sufferings; Lady Ottoline vicariously sought just such "experiences of the soul." James may have been right about the wife—a "good-looking fat creature, an excellent cook"—but he was otherwise mistaken. Conrad's mysterious eyes suggested untold adventures and experiences. He could have understood her, if he'd chosen to.

But he did not so choose. Instead, at afternoon's end Conrad accompanied Lady Ottoline to the station and with a bow put her on the London train.

Charles Stewart Rolls
Henry Royce

IN 1899 THE HONOURABLE Charles Stewart Rolls, twenty-two years old, was apprehended by the London police for "driving furiously" and failing to employ a man with a red flag to walk in front of his autocar to warn pedestrians, as required by law. The year 1900, however, heralded a new age. The speed limit was raised from four to twelve miles per hour, and the flag-bearer was erased from the statutes. When the Duke and Duchess of York (later George V and Queen Mary) dropped in on Lord Llangattock at his Sussex estate, it was the peer's son, young Rolls, who drove them around in his shiny new Panhard.

Unmentioned in accounts of the day is the way in which the royal passengers were joggled by engine vibration and deafened by noisy exhaust. The Panhard's inadequacies were a constant source of anguish to Rolls, and when soon afterward he set up a kind of aristocratic auto dealership in London's West End, he lamented that the cars he sold were, although the best available, not comfortable, reliable, or English. English cars were an abomination.

Except perhaps for one currently being assembled in the North. There a certain Henry Royce had designed his way from abject poverty to the successful manufacture of dynamos and electric cranes. He was also the owner of a malfunctioning Decauville, and had vowed to build a car that worked. He had in mind a ten-horsepower, two-cylinder model, for which he continued to design improvements. Rolls heard of it through the grapevine; could Royce come to London to consult? Sorry, Royce was busy, but he would be glad to see Rolls in Manchester.

The natural aristocracy of genius won out: Rolls took the train north. They met in the Palm Court of the Midland Hotel early in May 1904. Working-class diction confronted Cambridge enunciation, but they spoke the same language; besides, they liked each other. After lunch they took a little spin. The new car purred along smoothly, quietly; nothing rattled, nothing broke. It was the best car in the world. Before long the world would know it.

Richard Nixon
Madame Mao

J IANG QING WAS NOT PLEASED that in this matter of inviting the president of the United States to visit China, her opposition had been overruled. She disapproved of her husband's rapprochement with the American Imperialist Devil. True, as a young actress in Shanghai in the 1930s, she had adored Hollywood films, copied Garbo in her dress, worn makeup, and adopted high heels, which posed problems, because her feet had been bound when she was a child. She had struggled against that bourgeois past ever since. Not to mention the bourgeois present—during the Cultural Revolution she had repeatedly vilified America. Here she was now, on a cold evening in February 1972, ushering into the Great Hall of the People (5,000 of them in attendance) President and Mrs. Nixon.

Jiang opted to be charming but aloof. If Pat Nixon's two-tone lavender gown outshone her own austere garb, it was still her night. *The Red Detachment of Women* was her show, a balletic fusion of song, dance, and political ideology that she, as the mistress of revolutionary theater, personally had created. The dancers raised their arms in fists instead of the usual delicately upturned palms. Jiang faced the man who had led the anti-China lobby for years. "Why," she asked disingenuously, "did you not come to China before now?"

Other questions were similarly double-barreled. Did the President share her enthusiasm for John Steinbeck? (What about the downtrodden Okie proletariat anyway?) Why had Jack London committed suicide? (Could he not stomach decadent capitalist values any longer?) When Nixon attempted to change the subject by asking Jiang the names of the writer, composer, and director of *Red Detachment*, she informed him graciously that it had been "created by the masses." He mustered up a smile.

Four eventful years passed. When Nixon returned to China, it was as a private citizen; by his third visit Jiang Qing, too, had fallen from power. The fact that she, however, was in prison left Nixon more convinced than ever of the superiority of the capitalist system.

John L. Sullivan

Alfred I. du Pont

BAREKNUCKLE PRIZEFIGHTING was an illegal sport in the 1880s, but the new heavyweight champion was nonetheless a national hero. He took the role seriously: after each win he would raise his celebrated right arm and in sonorous tones assure his fans that he could whip any man "born of woman," or "in the house," or "breathing," and then conclude, "Thanking you one and all very kindly, I remain, yours truly, John L. Sullivan."

That winter of 1883, Sullivan appeared at Howard's Athenaeum, a Boston burlesque house, where he took on all comers for a prize of $1,000. Most were first-generation Irish-American street toughs like him, but one evening his contender was a handsome, blond young man who said that he was Alfred I. du Pont, a freshman at MIT, and that he was there because his allowance of thirty dollars a month was inadequate. John L. was sympathetic. His nightly bar bills were bigger than that. Besides, he admired book learning. So he sparred with Alfred I. over sufficient rounds to ensure him the fifty-dollar consolation prize.

But this was no one-fight stand. Although a du Pont, Alfred I. had grown up among the workers in the black-powder mills; like their children, he had learned to settle all disputes with his fists. He felt drawn to the expansive, generous Sullivan, only six years his senior, who in turn gave him pointers for the ring, debated the newly introduced Marquess of Queensbury rules, and kept him by his side through long evenings in local saloons. That Alfred I. was the eldest son of the eldest son of the eldest son of the founder of E. I. du Pont de Nemours was of no consequence.

In time John L. was defeated and shifted his talents to the New York stage. Alfred I., in town from Delaware, would attend; on learning of his presence, Sullivan would interrupt the melodrama, advance to the footlights, and thunder out, "My greetings to Mr. Alfred I. du Pont!" And by John L.'s final round it didn't matter that he had drunk up or given away all that prize money, because Alfred I. provided a monthly pension and a little farm in Massachusetts for his friend.

Yvette Guilbert

Henri de Toulouse-Lautrec

FOR A DECADE Lautrec drew the dancing girls of Montmartre with their long, graceful legs—so unlike his own. But by 1894, the year he turned thirty, the freshness was off the Moulin Rouge, and fashionable nightlife had moved back into the heart of Paris. A tall redhead with a ski-jump nose and thin arms encased in long black gloves half sang, half recited her bawdy songs in *cafés-concerts*. Yvette Guilbert, the daughter of a seamstress, was an immense success, and the scion of counts of Toulouse and viscounts of Lautrec went often to see her.

Perhaps he fell in love. Yvette was not beautiful—she had, he said, the "profile of a guttersnipe swan"—but singularity attracted him. He designed a poster for her and sent her the sketch—a perfect (and therefore unflattering) likeness that her friends insisted she turn down. "Another time," she wrote him consolingly. "But don't make me so appallingly ugly! Just a little less!"

Encouraged, Lautrec proposed an album of lithographs devoted entirely to her. That spring, accompanied by the dramatist Maurice Donnay, he came to lunch in the avenue de Villiers to discuss it. Yvette was prepared for his stuntedness but not, she wrote later, for the "huge dark head . . . the nose broad enough for two faces, and a mouth that gashed the face from cheek to cheek." But the eyes behind the spectacles were "astonishingly, luminously bright." She worried about how he would get onto his chair, which had no rungs. At lunch his chin was only eight inches above the tablecloth, and food seemed simply to vanish in his cavernous mouth, but he was such good company that she succumbed to his charm.

Later she became better acquainted with his acerbic side. In the course of their friendship Lautrec mocked her romantic inclinations; Yvette, in turn, castigated him for drinking to excess and living, by preference, in a brothel. The lithographs were widely praised, but it miffed her that he exaggerated the grotesque. "Really," she said, unthinking, "you have a genius for depicting deformity!" "But of course," he replied.

Fred Astaire

Count Basie

BASIE, OF COURSE, wasn't baptized "Count." Neither was Astaire born "Astaire"—his family name was Austerlitz. Of Omaha, yet. Basie—William, that is—came by his title during his jazz apprenticeship in Kansas City. He'd often miss a work session, and the bandleader Bennie Moten would storm, "Where is that no-'count Basie?" Where, indeed? Bill Basie, won't you please . . .

Which is not to say that he wasn't a prince of a fellow, and Astaire, too. When they met, in New York, in the summer of 1960, to discuss the forthcoming TV special *Astaire Time,* it was like one royal to another. Astaire received him, Basie recalled, in his suite at the St. Regis. "Well, Count Basie! So nice to . . . I'm so happy we could . . . I've been looking forward to . . ." and then a little conversation about building a dance around "Sweet Georgia Brown." "You got it!" Basie said.

Astaire remembered it otherwise—each of them deferring to the other. "You just play and I'll dance," he suggested. "No, no," Basie said, "you dance and I'll play."

There are also two versions of what happened next. The way Basie told it, he flew out to California, went directly to Astaire, and handed him the tape of "Sweet Georgia Brown." It was put on the machine, and Astaire started dancing. Not so, Astaire said. According to him, the plane landed; Basie was due at rehearsal, and then overdue. Seems he hightailed it out to the racetrack. Didn't show up till the next morning. "Well, man," he said, "I'm right outta money. Could you slip me five hundred?"

Astaire did—the money didn't matter—but to him rehearsals were sacrosanct. At sixty-one he still worked hard to make dance look easy. And, as he told it, the Count played hooky again—and again lost! But Astaire was patient. He liked the turf himself; besides, he'd yearned for years to do the blues with Basie. He loaned him his box at the track *and* his chauffeur and, after Basie had played the ponies, fetched him back to play the piano. At the keys the Count was always a winner. And Astaire never lost a dance.

J. P. Morgan
Kaiser Wilhelm II

ONE REASON for Pierpont Morgan's European trip that summer of 1902 was to attend the coronation of his friend Edward VII. Another was to meet Edward's nephew, Kaiser Wilhelm II. The Kaiser, Morgan knew, was a different animal entirely from Edward and himself, whose proper public lives shielded considerable private indecorum. Kaiser Wilhelm was younger, fitter, and on the surface less inhibited, but underneath he was a straitlaced, puritanical Prussian.

Morgan's purpose for the meeting was twofold. He had in mind to add the Kaiser to the string of European princes whom he dined with, advised on monetary matters, and quietly funded when they found themselves financially embarrassed. But there was also a deal afoot. With an international marine cartel in mind, Morgan had recently bought the British White Star Line and was casting covetous glances at Germany's Hamburg-American. So in July he boarded his magnificent steam yacht *Corsair III* and set off for the annual regatta at Kiel.

Morgan understood that the Kaiser would be overseeing the races from the imperial *Hohenzollern*. Would he come to lunch? Wilhelm accepted. With his sixty-nine-man crew at attention, Morgan welcomed the Kaiser aboard and introduced him to his guests, including the beautiful actress Maxine Elliott, who was his mistress, although that wasn't mentioned. At table those in the royal retinue tried to avoid staring at their host's large, inflamed nose, and those in Morgan's entourage at the guest of honor's withered left hand. When afterward Wilhelm proposed a brisk turn about the quarterdeck, the portly Pierpont, who hated exercise, thought it politic to concur.

Later Morgan and his new friend dined together in private. But Wilhelm adored his navy and, by extension, his merchant marine, and the sale of the Hamburg-American was delicately sidestepped. Morgan had to return home without his deal. Still, he counted the summer a success. "I have met the Kaiser," he informed the press, "and I like him."

J. K. Galbraith

J. M. Keynes

Somewhat to his surprise, John Kenneth Galbraith—a young man from rural Canada with a Ph.D. in economics—found himself in Washington, in charge of price controls for the entire United States. The job of "price czar" was a thankless one, but it commanded a degree of power from which, he would later say, the rest of his life was all downhill. One busy day in the late spring of 1942 his secretary announced that a "Mr. Kines" wanted to see him. The name stirred no recognition, and Galbraith told her to put him off. The secretary persisted: "I have the feeling that Mr. Kines somehow *expects* you to see him." Realization dawned: "Kines" was "Kanes"—that is, Keynes. Galbraith felt, he said, like a parish priest who has the pope in his outer office.

John Maynard Keynes was the guru of the new economics. Galbraith and other young enthusiasts heralded his concept of state responsibility for economic management, even to the extent of deficit spending, as revolutionary (American businessmen said heretical), and appointed themselves his disciples. Galbraith had gone to Cambridge intending to study under him, but Keynes was recovering from a heart attack and did not teach that year.

Now he had materialized in Galbraith's office, quite without fanfare. Keynes came right to the point, which was hogs and corn—or as he termed it, pigs and fodder. He had brought along "A Memorandum on the Pig/Pig Fodder Ratio," and he was anxious to talk about the very important matter of how to price corn in relation to hogs to avoid wasted grain but still ensure an adequate supply of pork. Keynes was ever the pragmatist. As bursar of King's College, he regularly oversaw the farming of college land, studied the finer points of livestock, and attended pig sales, and he had even tried breeding.

Any semblance of work was abandoned that day. Later there would be discussions of a more arcane nature, but Galbraith never forgot that on this first occasion he and Keynes met not as the young price czar and the most influential economist of the century, but as an ex-farmboy and his much-admired mentor, who just happened to run a pig farm on the side.

Jean Renoir

Erich von Stroheim

B Y THE MID-1930S the Austrian émigré actor-director Erich von Stroheim was anathema to the entire Hollywood establishment. They inveighed against his wildly extravagant and dictatorial practices and his increasing bent for decadent sensuality. So he cut out for Paris. The admiring French showered him with acting opportunities. The director Jean Renoir, who as a young man had sat through von Stroheim's *Foolish Wives* thirty-four times and lauded the stark realism of *Greed,* sent him a new script about French soldiers in a German POW camp during the First World War— *La Grande Illusion.*

A meeting was arranged. As von Stroheim waited stiffly in a makeshift office, a cherubic man wearing a baggy suit appeared at the door. Renoir was unaware of his prospective actor's abhorrence of bodily contact with members of his own sex (on occasion von Stroheim employed a click of the heels to avoid shaking hands), and in the best Gallic style kissed him firmly on both cheeks. Von Stroheim tensed, but the gesture was so heartfelt that not only did he succumb, he returned it in kind.

He was less yielding where his film image was concerned. Hardly had conversation begun when von Stroheim was making suggestions about the script—such as combining the two German officer roles into one, for himself. Later he pressed for a more flamboyant uniform. Only when shooting began and he wanted to incorporate prostitutes into the opening scene did Renoir balk. Von Stroheim's combat experience had, after all, been limited to playing granite-faced Huns on the silver screen. It was Renoir who had fought in the trenches and frequented the frontline officers' mess—*sans* prostitutes. How could his idol of cinematic realism opt for clichés of that sort?

Once again von Stroheim had embroiled himself in a test of wills, but this time his adversary, instead of pulling rank or dismissing him, burst into tears. He would give up the film rather than quarrel, Renoir said. No, no, replied a repentant von Stroheim; from now on he would follow instructions with slavish docility. Wet-eyed, they fell into each other's arms, protesting eternal *entente* and *Freundschaft* forever.

Isak Dinesen
Marilyn Monroe

On the fifth of February, 1959, Carson McCullers gave a luncheon. She seldom entertained anymore, her health was so precarious, but Isak Dinesen was in town—New York, that is—for the first (and only) time, and there were two women she wanted to meet. McCullers was one. The other was Marilyn Monroe.

Dinesen mentioned this to McCullers when they were introduced at a literary function, and Carson said nothing could be easier. She knew Marilyn, she said, and there was Arthur Miller at the next table; she would ask a few old friends as well. It was a little disconcerting to learn that "Tanya," as Dinesen preferred being called, lived on oysters and white grapes, washed down with champagne—so perhaps a soufflé, too, McCullers told her cook, in case the other guests found that fare meager.

On the day, the Millers called for Dinesen in their car, late—when was it otherwise with Marilyn? But Monroe did look luscious in her black sheath with the pronounced décolletage and fur collar. Tanya, who weighed eighty-odd pounds, wore an elegant gray suit, her head swathed in a turban. After lunch she told one of her tales—about being young in Kenya and killing her first lion and sending the skin to the King of Denmark. It was a hard act to follow. But Marilyn had a story, too, if a less heroic one: She was giving a dinner party, using her mother-in-law's recipe for noodles, but it got late, the guests arrived, and she had to finish off the noodles with a hair dryer. Marilyn was always best in comic parts. Then Carson, as she told it later, put a record on the phonograph, and she, Tanya, and Marilyn danced together—on top of the black marble dining table, she said.

Blame it on the oysters and champagne. Illusion prevailed that day. Karen Blixen and Norma Jean Baker were submerged in the myths of Dinesen and Monroe. Marilyn had not disappointed Dinesen, who compared her to a lion cub, all unbounded vitality and innocence. There was a natural sympathy between them; McCullers, watching them, even called it love.

George S. Patton
Bill Mauldin

THEY WERE NOT FIGHTING the same war. General Patton's was a conflict of calculated maneuvers by superbly trained troops toward a defined goal: a dash for glory while in pursuit of victory. Sergeant Mauldin's was a war of rain and mud and barbed wire, all the squalid actualities of the Italian campaign. The fact that Mauldin was not yet twenty-five and carried a pen and sketch pad instead of a gun did not dull that perception. His cartoons in *Stars and Stripes* came out of this war, and Willie and Joe, his antiheroes, were unshaven, grubby dogfaces. Mauldin reserved his barbs for the top brass and the MPs. For this he was accused of undermining morale.

But what made Patton choleric was the way Willie and Joe *looked*. Scruffy. Disheveled. His own Third Army troops were clean-shaven, boots polished, neckties in place. Why, he sputtered to the Supreme Command, should *Stars and Stripes* star Willie and Joe?

Then, early in 1945, Mauldin strayed up to Paris, where he was pounced upon by that same Supreme Command and packed off to Third Army headquarters, in Luxembourg's royal palace, to "talk it over" with Patton. There in his office, armed with ivory-handled pistol and ready invective, Patton launched into a diatribe on Mauldin's goddamn bums, no respect for the Army, was he trying to incite a goddamn mutiny? Then came a long harangue on the importance of rank through four thousand years of military history. Mauldin was permitted about a minute and a half to state his case, that his cartoons were a safety valve for the disgruntlement of the average soldier, before he was attacked again for allowing his characters to "bitch and beef and gripe and run around with beards on their faces." "I guess we understand each other now," Patton concluded, and Mauldin was dismissed.

Nothing changed, of course, but then, the war was winding down. In March, Patton crossed the Rhine. In May, Mauldin won a Pulitzer. By June both were back in the States, and there on the cover of *Time* was Willie. He, too, was coming home.

Andrew Mellon

Joseph Duveen

WHEN IN LONDON, the art dealer Joseph Duveen stayed at Claridge's. His luxurious fourth-floor suite was graced with his latest acquisitions in pre nineteenth-century art, in transition between the great houses of Europe and their American counterparts. There the voluble Duveen received titled ladies and an occasional Yankee millionaire. But by 1921 super-rich Americans with a taste for Old Masters were in short supply. J. P. Morgan was dead, as was Henry Clay Frick, while Andrew Mellon patronized the rival gallery, Knoedler's.

The problem for the proprietor of Duveen Brothers, New York, was to meet Mr. Mellon of Pittsburgh, now also of Washington, where he ran the Treasury. Once Duveen found himself on the same transatlantic crossing as Mellon. He tipped the steward handsomely to place their deck chairs side by side, but although every day he reclined expectantly in his, the taciturn Mellon only paced the deck and retired to his cabin.

Then, during one sojourn at Claridge's, Duveen's valet reported that he had met Mellon's valet, currently residing with his master on the third floor. Duveen plotted his campaign. He had himself moved down to two, and discreetly solicited intelligence from above. One afternoon Mellon's valet telephoned that his master was about to go out for a stroll. Duveen reached for his hat and coat. As the lift descended from the third floor to halt at the second, he stepped in with an air of surprised pleasure. "How do you do, Mr. Mellon," he said.

The upshot was that Mellon walked not in the park that day but in the National Gallery, where he was favored with his companion's views on the paintings. On the way back to the hotel, Mellon learned that his companion, too, possessed a number of Old Masters—fewer than the museum had, of course, but of like quality and, it was merely hinted, available. In the aftermath much art exchanged hands, and later another National Gallery was built, this time in Washington, to house Duveen's . . . Mellon's . . . now the nation's . . . Old Masters.

Irving Berlin

George Gershwin

THE GREAT WAR was over, and the whole country seemed addicted to song. Who better to supply the national need than the King of Ragtime, Irving Berlin? "Come on and hear (*boom! boom!*), come on and hear (*boom! boom!*) Alexander's Ragtime Band." That early hit had sold a million copies in a few months. Now Berlin, back from the Army, stopped by the T. B. Harms Co., in Tin Pan Alley, to show the publisher Max Dreyfus his latest. "That Revolutionary Rag," Dreyfus read, "'Twas made across the sea / By a tricky slicky / Bolsheviki . . ." But the notes were a problem. Berlin's musical education had evolved from a battered piano in a Bowery saloon and remained forever locked in the key of F sharp. He needed someone to take down the song for him. Dreyfus said he had just the man—only a kid, really, but showing great promise.

Enter young George Gershwin, glad to oblige. Harms was a big step up from Remick, where he had pounded a piano in a cubicle as many as ten hours a day. He took down the song, made a lead sheet, and played it back to Berlin with extravagant improvisations that left it almost unrecognizable. Then, abruptly, he asked the composer for a job as his musical secretary. Berlin intimated he might be overqualified. What did he really want to do? Write songs, Gershwin said, tearing up the keyboard with his latest. "What the hell do you want to work for anyone else for?" Berlin asked. "Work for yourself!"

Gershwin took his advice, and within the year there was "Swanee." Then came "Stairway to Paradise." "Rhapsody in Blue" made him as famous, and almost as wealthy, as Berlin. They became friends—two hustlers of Russian-Jewish parentage making it big in America.

Gershwin was twenty that day they met in the Alley. Brash, confident, he seemed just at the beginning of his life, whereas in reality it was more than half over. Berlin, a more cautious thirty, would not have believed his own eventual longevity. Surely Alexander did strike up the band the day Irving Berlin reached one hundred!

Gertrude Stein

Edith Sitwell

THIS IS IN FACT A FIRST, middle, and (arguably) final encounter. The story begins in 1924, when Edith Sitwell came to Paris and called at 27, rue de Fleurus, where Gertrude Stein and Alice B. Toklas lived and Cézannes and Picassos hung on the walls. Stein's expectations were guarded: Sitwell had discussed her work in English journals, not always with enthusiasm. But Stein's impression was favorable. Edith Sitwell was very tall, Gertrude noted—beautiful, with a most distinguished nose, and she walked as if advancing and withdrawing at the same time. Alice recalled a double-breasted coat with large buttons. Edith likened Gertrude to an Easter Island idol. They talked about poetry: Sitwell's unorthodox, mocking poems shocked the public as much as did Stein's prose. Edith admired Gertrude's prose—how she "threw a word into the air," freeing it of past associations.

More visits were exchanged, and on her return home Sitwell lobbied for Stein to lecture at Cambridge and Oxford. This was arranged, and Edith, with her brothers Osbert and Sacheverell, went in escort, aristocratic cranes in attendance on a plump partridge. To Edith's embarrassment, Gertrude closed the Oxford lecture with her word portrait "Sitwell Edith Sitwell," which began, "Introduces have and heard. Miss Edith Sitwell have and heard," and continued in kind.

Perhaps more rivalry existed than either cared to confront. Some years later in Paris, Sitwell was asked by Sylvia Beach, the proprietor of the bookshop Shakespeare and Company, to speak at one of her "evenings" on the subject of Gertrude Stein. At nine o'clock the literary *monde*—Gertrude and Alice included—gathered in anticipation. Edith looked coolly down her aquiline nose, placed the tips of her long white fingers together, and recited a little Shakespeare. She moved on to other Elizabethans. Then she read from her own poetry. The evening ended without a mention of Gertrude Stein. Miss Edith Sitwell had been heard.

At Yasnaya Polyana, 1895

Edward Sorel

Anton Chekhov
Leo Tolstoy

CHEKHOV HAD BEEN LIVING at Melikhovo, in Moscow province, for three years, and still he resisted suggestions that he call at nearby Yasnaya Polyana. He said he was busy. As a fledgling landowner, he was putting his farm in order; as a doctor, he treated the peasants. He repaired the church, built schools. His stories supported all these activities and brought wide critical acclaim. They were the credentials he would take with him when he went to meet Count Tolstoy—he, Anton Pavlovich, son of a failed grocer, grandson of a serf.

It was August 1895 when Chekhov at last set off for Yasnaya Polyana. He arrived just as the master, in his linen peasant blouse, was on his way to bathe in the stream. Chekhov must come along. Tolstoy undressed at the bathhouse and plunged into the water. Immersed up to his neck, his white beard floating on the surface, he conversed with his guest. That evening passages from the first draft of *Resurrection* were read aloud. Chekhov spent the night; he felt comfortable at Yasnaya Polyana.

Tolstoy admitted he liked Chekhov, but thought he lacked a point of view. Clearly, Chekhov had suppressed his own opinions, which were antipodal to those of his host. Tolstoy held that the salvation of Russia lay in discarding the accoutrements of civilization and returning to the life of the soil. He was opposed to higher education, to holding property, even to the practice of medicine.

Later Chekhov would satirize this dubious ideology in his own stories, and at subsequent meetings the two men would argue their disparate philosophies. Chekhov hated the moralizing in Tolstoy's novels; Tolstoy condemned Chekhov's plays as worse than Shakespeare's. But something elemental had happened by the stream at Yasnaya Polyana. Engulfed in his own last illness, Chekhov worried about Tolstoy's health. He referred to him as that "crafty old man" but acknowledged that he never loved another as well. "While there is a Tolstoy in literature," Chekhov said, "it is pleasant and agreeable to be a writer."

Charles de Gaulle

Franklin D. Roosevelt

I N 1940, GENERAL DE GAULLE escaped Nazi-occupied France for England and declared himself head of the Free French forces there. He insisted, in defiance of realities, that the Third Republic had not succumbed with the fall of France but was alive and well in London, under his personal protection. He spoke of himself as the soul of France. In Washington, President Roosevelt scoffed. A time-and-again veteran of the American electoral process, he found such arrogation of titular authority, as if by divine right, galling. The general—a mere *brigadier*—had no mandate from his people. An *arriviste,* in Roosevelt's view.

But by 1943, Allied landings in French North Africa forced the issue of who should govern the liberated territories. Roosevelt settled on stuffy but malleable General Giraud. He was irate that both the French Resistance and the American public preferred de Gaulle—thus compelling him, when he met with Churchill at Anfa near Casablanca in January, to invite both generals along.

De Gaulle arrived, towering, touchy. He grumbled at the barbed wire and bayonets, and American sentries on what he considered French soil. That evening he was conducted to Roosevelt's villa, where, on invitation, he sat stiffly on a couch beside his host. The president opened the dialogue in colloquial French. The general replied in the classic speech of the *philosophes.* Interpreters had to be called in, and they augmented the confusion. Roosevelt next tried graciousness and charm, but charm is difficult to translate, and the graciousness was belied by ominous presences in the upper gallery, bulging drapery, and the unmistakable outline of a tommy gun.

De Gaulle viewed the episode as hostile to him and, by extension, to France. He was intransigent on the subject of his own preeminence, and when Roosevelt, with his own Dutch stubbornness, high-handedly announced that he could not back de Gaulle because France had not elected him, de Gaulle replied unblinking that Joan of Arc had not been elected either.

Oscar Wilde

Walt Whitman

WRAPPED IN HIS fur-trimmed green greatcoat, the young poet Oscar Wilde arrived in America for a lecture tour in January 1882. He came as the exponent of aestheticism to a puritanical and often hostile people. But cosmopolitan New York lionized him, and the press loved him: his flamboyance was good copy. In Philadelphia, his second stop, he mentioned that he did "so hope to meet Mr. Whitman." A card promptly arrived: "Walt Whitman will be in from 2 till 3½ this afternoon."

Whitman lived very simply in nearby Camden with his brother and sister-in-law. Like Wilde, he was tall and solidly built, but his rough homespun suit and open shirt were in sharp contrast to his visitor's sartorial elegance. "I come as a poet to call upon a poet," Wilde intoned in greeting. He then described how his mother had read *Leaves of Grass* aloud to him as a child. Pleased, Whitman produced a bottle of his sister-in-law's elderberry wine and invited his guest to help consume it. "I will call you Oscar," he said.

The bottle emptied, they adjourned to the den—to be on "thee and thou terms," as Whitman put it. Wilde asked about his theory of composition. He had once been a typesetter, Whitman explained, and aimed at making his verse "look all neat and pretty on the pages, like the epitaph on a square tombstone." But to advocate beauty and charm over substance, as in Wilde's aestheticism— that was going too far. "Why, Oscar," Whitman objected, "it always seems to me that the fellow who makes a dead set at beauty by itself is in a bad way."

To Whitman, however, Wilde was never such a fellow. With him Wilde had dropped his affectations and found no occasion for his famed barbed wit; his Oscar was always "a fine large handsome youngster." As for Wilde, he remembered the afternoon in terms of fresh air and sunlight, and when a friend, knowing his tastes, remarked that the elderberry wine must have been difficult to get down, he replied, "If it had been vinegar, I should have drunk it all the same."

Jean-Paul Marat
Charlotte Corday

IT WAS JULY 1793—four years after the fall of the Bastille and some six months since the king's execution. To Charlotte Corday, in Caen, as to many others in the provinces, the promise of the Revolution had been irretrievably tarnished. The excesses of the Jacobins were to blame. Even in Girondist Caen there was a guillotine now: its first victim was the priest who years before had attended Charlotte's mother when she died in childbirth. And as Corday knew, no Jacobin in France more avidly promoted the guillotine, or unmasked more "traitors," than the virulent polemicist and pamphleteer Jean-Paul Marat.

So when she read exhortations like "Let Marat's head fall and the Republic is saved!" posted along the streets of Caen, Corday—a young and beautiful descendant of the dramatist Corneille—rose to claim her destined role. On July 9 she boarded the Paris coach. On the morning of the thirteenth she walked from her lodgings to the Palais Royal and along the way bought a newspaper, a black hat with green ribbons, and a large kitchen knife. After one abortive attempt she managed to slip into the house she sought, on the rue des Cordeliers, and then, by loudly declaring that she bore valuable information, to confront Marat himself.

Marat lay, as he had for weeks, in his shoe-shaped tub, attempting with solutions of kaolin to relieve the scaly sores that afflicted his body. A board served as his desk. His receiving *en bain* had the advantage that his broad shoulders and brawny arms were fully visible while his almost stunted lower body was not. As she sat at his side, Charlotte described the rebellious atmosphere at Caen. Asked for names, she coolly ticked them off. Marat was pleased. "In a few days I will have them all guillotined," he said, and thereby made easier what followed. Like the tragedienne she saw herself, Charlotte Corday stood erect, pulled the knife from her bodice, and aimed true.

Joseph Haydn
Lady Emma Hamilton

B Y THE SUMMER of 1800, Napoleon had made travel about Europe precarious in the extreme. Sir William Hamilton, the seasoned British ambassador to Naples, his wife, Emma, and Lord Admiral Horatio Nelson, en route as a threesome from Sicily to England, found themselves deflected to Vienna. They were feeling their age and condition. The Lord Admiral had lost an arm, most of his upper teeth, and the use of one eye; Sir William was chronically ill; and the once classically beautiful Emma—painted by Romney, Lawrence, and Reynolds—had put on weight, only partially as a result of her being (secretly) five months pregnant with Nelson's child. From Vienna they went to join the Prince and Princess Esterházy at nearby Eisenstadt.

The chief attraction of Eisenstadt was, of course, that Haydn lived there. Kapellmeister under a succession of Esterházys, he conducted his little orchestra, mothered his young musicians, and created his rich harmonies and buoyant melodies. He also had enjoyed two highly satisfactory sojourns in England—the London symphonies attest to that. Now he welcomed these illustrious, if oddly matched, English guests, and sent to Vienna for the score of his cantata *Arianna a Naxos,* in which Emma had expressed particular interest.

Not since her early days in Naples, when the singing master came three times a day and household servants doubled as fiddlers, had Emma been so completely surrounded by music. Esterházy provided a partridge shoot, fireworks, and a ball as well, but music reigned. At one concert, to Haydn's accompaniment, Emma sang the alto aria from *Arianna;* critical assessment of her voice varied, but the audience was ecstatic. Haydn rewarded her with the manuscripts of two of his English songs. Clearly, he was taken with her beauty; perhaps, too, her presence recalled a certain London romance still warm in his memory. If he knew of her dubious past, or suspected her unconventional present, he gave no sign.

H. L. Mencken
Theodore Dreiser

I N 1907 THE AUTHOR of *Sister Carrie*, widely considered the most degenerate novel of the decade, was employed by the Butterick Publishing Company of New York in the improbable role of editor of their trio of genteel women's magazines. From a desk the size of a billiard table, in an office of comparable scale, Dreiser acquired the lachrymose poetry and lackluster fiction that filled the pages of *The Delineator*. At one point a ghostwriter was needed for a series on the care and feeding of babies, and a versatile young writer for *The Baltimore Sun*, Henry L. Mencken, was approached. Mencken accepted the assignment. In short order, pieces on crying babies and nursing mothers were making their way from the bachelor Mencken to the childless Dreiser for approval.

On a summer day the following year, Mencken presented himself at the Butterick offices, decked out, Dreiser recalled, in yellow shoes and a bright tie, and reminding him of a petted and possibly overfinanced brewer's son. "Well, well," Dreiser said, "if it isn't Anheuser's own brightest boy out to see the town"—a joshing that Mencken seized upon with delight, although in fact his father, a cigar manufacturer, had been dead nearly ten years. Then, from the depths of an oversize chair intended to discomfit cocky neophytes, Mencken beamed at his editor and proceeded to charm him with trenchant observations on the American scene.

Years of epistolary and beer-hall camaraderie followed. Butterick fired Dreiser, and Mencken, having catapulted into fame as a newspaperman, editor, and critic, took on as well the role of public defender of the lumbering, contentious novelist. They shared an antipathy for convention, and only later did Dreiser's defects of style—both life and literary—erode Mencken's allegiance. The break came when Mencken labeled *An American Tragedy* "a colossal botch." Still, as Dreiser neared death he wrote to thank Mencken for helping fight the good fight. "What you forget," Mencken replied, "is how we both enjoyed the battle."

Benito Mussolini
Adolf Hitler

As HIS PLANE PUT DOWN in Venice on June 14, 1934, Adolf Hitler felt himself at a decided disadvantage. For one thing, he had neglected to wear a uniform. It was he who had requested the meeting, but still new to dictatorship, he had not foreseen that his brown gabardine and limp fedora would be overshadowed by the snappy attire of the commander in chief of the Italian Fascist militia. Then there were the facts that Mussolini spoke German, while he himself did not know Italian, and that this was foreign territory. In spite of stiff-armed salutes, heel-clicking, and the "Horst Wessel Song," Hitler could not quite control a nervous twitch.

For his part, Mussolini planned to be a perfect host. He had the confidence of a man who, after declaring himself minister of war, the navy, and the air force, *then* learned to swim and fly, and to ride a horse so that he could review his troops. Neither he nor Hitler had risen above the rank of corporal in the last war, but there was no need to bring that up. It was the fate of Austria that Mussolini wished to discuss. To that end, he conducted his guest by car to Strà, near Padua, where they secluded themselves in the drawing room of the royal palace.

At that point all formality—and civility—ceased. Opposition brought out the maniacal in Hitler. "It is my will, and the indomitable will of the German people," screeched the Führer, "that Austria become an integral part of the Reich!" Il Duce blasted back with Italy's equally indomitable resolve that Austria remain independent. Anxious attendants heard fists thumping, and increasingly frenzied rantings. Finally the door flew open and both men tramped through. They did not look at each other. They acknowledged the cheering crowd and returned to Venice in separate cars.

Yet to be endured were formal dinners, a concert of Wagner, the obligatory military review. Good-byes were frigid. What was his impression? Mussolini was asked afterward. "A mad little clown," he said.

Suzanne Valadon

Erik Satie

ERIK SATIE was twenty-one and a Conservatoire dropout when he traded the bourgeois comfort of his parents' home for a ramshackle hole at the foot of Montmartre. It was late in 1887. He was just completing those hauntingly simple little *Gymnopédies,* and the new, unconventional tunes that crowded his mind demanded a more free-spirited existence.

It was at the Chat Noir, the cabaret where he took a job as second pianist, that he met Suzanne Valadon. Only a year older, but wise in the world's uncertainties, she had left school at age nine for a clothing sweatshop, had worked as a waitress, a pushcart vendor, and a groom in a livery stable, and had joined a circus. At sixteen she became an artist's model. Beautiful, exuding a wild vitality, she was painted and loved in turn by Puvis de Chavannes and Renoir, either of whom she was wont to credit with the paternity of her son, Maurice (Utrillo). When she herself began to draw, Toulouse-Lautrec hung her works on his walls, and Degas, the Master, praised them.

On the night in question Valadon was at a corner table with her current lover when Satie joined them. Within minutes he was entranced; before the hour was out he had proposed. The lover seemed no impediment, but the time—three a.m.—proved a problem. "An impossible time to get to the *mairie,*" Satie said later, adding regretfully, "After that it was always too late. She had too many things on her mind to get married."

The ensuing affair was like no other in Valadon's experience. They sailed toy boats in the Luxembourg Gardens. Satie brought her necklaces of sausages. All the while he was composing short atonal pieces such as *Three Real Boneless Preludes for a Dog,* which he performed in friends' studios with Valadon at his feet. She became domestic, mended his socks, cooked. Her first work in oils was a portrait of him. Then, abruptly, she left. On that day he wrote the first of many letters he would send her over thirty years, protesting a love that, unlike youth in Montmartre, was eternal.

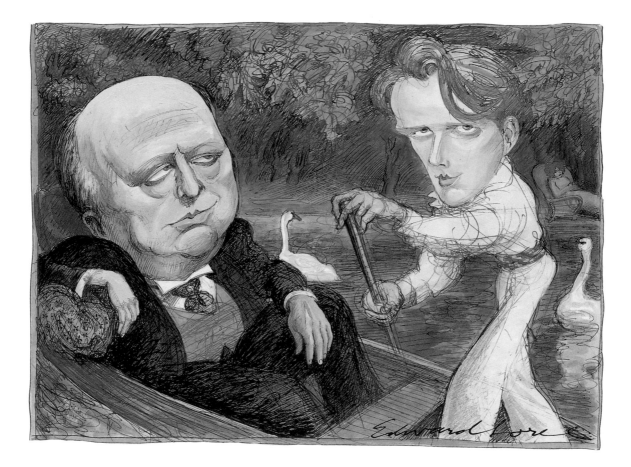

Henry James
_____
Rupert Brooke

FOR TWO DECADES young admirers—some English, some transplanted Americans such as he was—had clustered around Henry James. They are reflected (discreetly) in his stories. It was thus irregular but not entirely unexpected that an invitation to visit Cambridge in the spring of 1909 should come not from a don or a dean but from a few undergraduates and librarians. For James, who had spent a single (dull) year at Harvard nearly half a century before, the prospect of acting the "intellectual Pasha" within the ancient walls of this English Cambridge was not unwelcome.

The schedule proved formidable. There were breakfasts, tours, concerts, dinners, late-night bull sessions. New acolytes converged on each event, and James found himself not a little harried. Then, at lunch one day at Pembroke, he was introduced to a handsome young man from King's, Rupert Brooke—a poet, he was informed.

That James should eye Brooke in particular was not surprising. Everyone did. There was a careless grace about him, a sweetness, a radiance even. Was he thought of as a good poet? James asked his hosts later. He was not. "Thank goodness," the novelist remarked with his usual wry humor. "If he looked like that and was a good poet, too, I do not know what I should do."

On the final day of the visit, Brooke suggested a punt on the Cam. The corpulent James reclined on velvet cushions and, through half-closed eyes, admired alternately the small Palladian bridges and the loose-limbed young navigator before him, wearing white shirt and flannels and, in deference to his guest, shoes. Brooke's habitual undress and his inclination for moonlight bathing with friends of both sexes went unmentioned. Later he described the afternoon to a friend. "I did the fresh boyish stunt," he said, "and it was a great success."

As indeed it was. Six years later, when Brooke—by then a splendid sonneteer—died in the war, James, recalling that occasion when he had "very unforgettably met him," truly grieved.

August 1860 – Captain Richard Burton, explorer and
student of exotic sexual practice, travels to America
to meet with Brigham Young and learn about polygamy
among the Mormons.
He does not stay long.

Brigham Young
Captain Richard Burton

IN EARLY AUGUST 1860, Captain Richard Burton, lately of the Nile, crossed the Missouri and set off by mail wagon for Utah Territory. The American West was not his customary milieu. He was a man attracted to the forbidden and the exotic: Africa, Arabia, India were his usual haunts. He had learned strange languages and adopted stranger disguises to penetrate the shrines of Mecca and Medina, and had entered uninvited the holy city of Harar. A Victorian dissident, Burton appended his books of exploration with detailed descriptions of the marriage rites and sexual habits of native peoples. Polygamy fascinated him. He had crashed an Egyptian harem and, on another occasion, bedded down with the Bedouin. Now, in the New World, he was eager to visit the Mormon settlement at Salt Lake City. He particularly wanted to meet its leader, Brigham Young—this master carpenter turned high priest who had managed, in a puritanical and Christian country, to acquire twenty-two wives.

The "young rival" of the ancient holy cities lay before Burton in gridiron squares, remarkable for its symmetry. All was order. Burton was given an appointment for eleven a.m. in the prophet's office. The venerable sage he had expected was instead a heavyset but youngish man in gray homespun, who spoke with directness and occasional humor. Conversation touched on Burton's African explorations and on Utah and the agricultural, but could not be steered to the matrimonial. Young was firmly in control. Perhaps unexpectedly, the two men liked each other. Young took his visitor on a tour of the town, and Burton was impressed by the prophet's extensive holdings, especially the private school for his children and the "Lion House" for his plurality of wives. But the captain looked in vain for a veiled face glancing seductively from an upper window. Women were everywhere; what was missing was mystery. Mormon polygamy was, perhaps, simply the monotony of monogamy, multiplied.

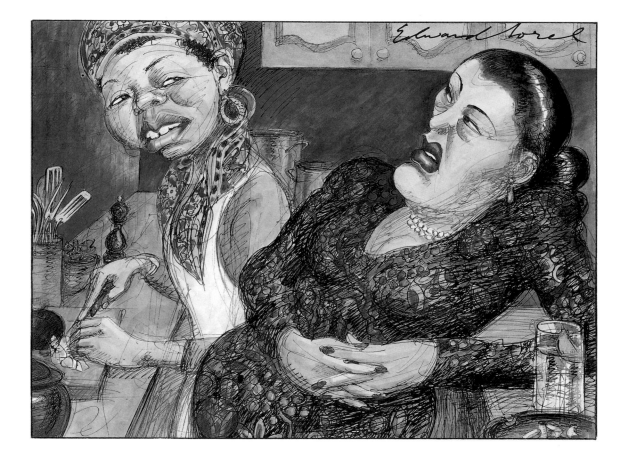

Maya Angelou
Billie Holiday

AFTER MAYA ANGELOU returned from her European tour as premier dancer in *Porgy and Bess,* she let her hair grow "natural," took a job as a nightclub singer, and moved with her son into a bungalow in Hollywood's swank Laurel Canyon. It was June 1958. One morning her voice coach, Frederick "Wilkie" Wilkerson, dropped by. Billie Holiday was in town; he would bring her over if Maya thought she could handle it. "What's to handle?" Angelou asked. "She's a woman. I'm a woman."

But her nonchalance quickly gave way to nerves. Billie Holiday was more than a woman; she was Lady Day, she was legend. She had teamed up with the greats—Lester Young, Benny Goodman, Count Basie—and broken ground as a black woman singer with an all-white band. Then there was the flip side—the dark past, the time served, the long addictions to drugs and alcohol, all too apparent in the ravaged figure now walking in the door.

At first Angelou found her guest hostile, her conversation a melee of sarcasm and obscenities. But after lunch—fried chicken, rice, Arkansas gravy—Holiday softened. Maya was a nice lady, and a good cook, too, she said. When Wilkerson got up to leave, she opted to stay. Angelou felt herself being watched. "You a square, ain't you?" Holiday said. Angelou admitted that she was.

Guy, aged twelve, came home from school. He was introduced, and proved charming. Holiday forgot that she couldn't stand children ("little crumbcrushers") and followed him out to water the lawn. She told him about all the low-down men she had known in her life, but she was careful to curb her profanity. After dinner she sang him a good-night song—"You're My Thrill."

Holiday spent five days with Angelou, and not until the end did she revert to her angry self. On the last evening she was abusive to Guy; she accompanied Maya to the nightclub and shouted her off the stage. Lady Day was some complicated woman. At parting she left Angelou with a two-edged prophecy: "You're going to be famous," she said. "But it won't be for singing."

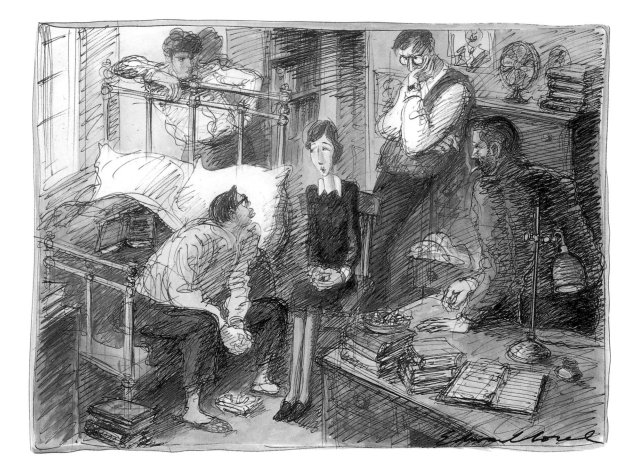

Jean-Paul Sartre
Simone de Beauvoir

SIMONE DE BEAUVOIR grew up in the closed society of proper bourgeois Paris, so to go to the Sorbonne at all, much less to study philosophy, was a hard-won success. To her father, philosophy was gibberish; her mother worried that she would lose her faith, overlooking the fact that this had already happened. Beauvoir knew she would have no dowry, ergo no husband; she should at least be able to choose her career.

By her third year she was acquainted with most of her fellow students, with the glaring exception of a young man of brilliant mind but dubious reputation (alcohol, women), Jean-Paul Sartre. Sartre and a few close friends shared a private language, heavy on the *bon mot sarcastique*, and they labeled Beauvoir "the badly dressed one with the beautiful blue eyes." Still, he knew she was expected to score very high on exams that he himself had failed the previous year, for not sticking to the subject. He sent her his drawing of Leibniz, the subject of her thesis, and asked to be introduced.

Toward that end Beauvoir was invited to a study session on a Monday morning in June 1929, in Sartre's room at the Cité Universitaire, for the purpose of expounding on Leibniz. She had long yearned to be included in this unorthodox group, and was terrified that they might find her "silly," although the one known for high jinks was Sartre. As host, however, he was reassuringly deferential. Shorter than Beauvoir, he wore a "more or less clean" shirt, she noted, and slippers. The room was a shambles: the bed unmade, ashtrays unemptied, books and papers everywhere. He escorted her ceremoniously to the only chair. She had barely started on Leibniz when the others declared him impossibly boring, but no one suggested that that was her fault, so she stayed for a discussion of Rousseau, interspersed with philosophical parodies by Sartre declaimed to Offenbach's music. It was a day that authenticated her dreams. A dowerless young woman had options other than marriage, of which the bourgeois life need never be a part.

Arthur Conan Doyle
Harry Houdini

ARTHUR CONAN DOYLE was obsessed from childhood with the supernatural. His Irish heritage, peopled with fairies and elves, prompted a dreamy acceptance of the insubstantial. Drawn to spiritualism, he attended his first séance at age twenty—about the time he was studying medicine, and seven years before Sherlock Holmes and Dr. Watson appeared on the scene.

In America, Ehrich Weiss, alias Harry Houdini, fifth son of a Hungarian rabbi, also tried séances at an early age. He was fascinated by illusion, but of the magical rather than the otherworldly kind. He began with simple conjury, and then perfected his own specialty—the artistry of escape.

Both men attained enormous celebrity. The creator of Holmes was knighted, and Houdini became the king of magic. In 1920 the latter was touring Britain, performing such breathtaking stunts as climbing out of locked trunks and straitjackets. Conan Doyle, now a convinced spiritualist, went to Portsmouth to see him and was dazzled by his almost swami-like discipline. He saw Houdini as another form of spiritualist, and after the show hurried backstage. The ruddy six-foot-four writer and the small, wiry magician met as seekers into the mystical. They talked for hours.

The two men corresponded often and hobnobbed when Sir Arthur came to America to lecture on spiritualism. Houdini was too impressed by his friend's distinction and sincerity to disclose that in his experience, mediums were charlatans and their practices sheer deviltry. He tried to explain how certain spooky tricks were done, but Conan Doyle would not listen. Perhaps Houdini should not have listened when Lady Conan Doyle suggested that they try to contact his beloved deceased mother—but in fact he missed her terribly and could not resist. As he and Sir Arthur sat in strained expectancy, Lady Conan Doyle, in a kind of trance, called for a message from Mother Weiss and took it down verbatim—as the spirit moved her. Sir Arthur thought the event a great success. But Houdini knew it was not: the message was in English—a language his Yiddish-speaking mama had never mastered.

Alexander Fleming

Marlene Dietrich

ON A DAY IN 1928 that was not unlike any other, a spore drifted in the open window of Alexander Fleming's laboratory at St. Mary's Hospital, London, and landed in a petri dish containing a culture of staphylococci. In time mold growth from the spore dissolved the staphylococci. This startling development impelled Fleming—ever attuned to the habits of his microbes—to new experimentation, from which emerged the identification of penicillin. Its later production as an antibiotic came just in time to save the lives of thousands of soldiers during the Second World War.

Marlene Dietrich witnessed its success firsthand. The glamorous German-born émigré to Hollywood spent the last year of the war at the European front, singing for the GIs. What she observed in field hospitals elevated Fleming to hero status in her eyes. If she could but see him . . . , she mentioned to the songwriter Mischa Spoliansky, in London, some five years later. Nothing easier, he replied. A small dinner party could be arranged—she had only to prepare the meal. Dietrich was delighted; she liked nothing better than to watch people she loved eat what she cooked. She wired her friend Erich Maria Remarque in New York for advice as to wines.

Fleming arrived at the Spolianskys' promptly at eight. That this dour Scot was no conversationalist became distressingly apparent over dinner. Dietrich was determined to avoid the subject of penicillin, but found herself groping for alternatives. The lovingly prepared food, the carefully selected wines were consumed by him without comment. Not until they were settled afterward in the living room did everyone relax. Talk turned to the great success of Spoliansky's songs. Fleming hummed a few bars from "Tonight or Never," even dropping in a word or two. Perhaps, Dietrich thought, the evening had not been a failure after all. But she was not sure until Fleming, reaching into the pocket of his jacket, blurted out, "That's the only thing I thought I could give you: the first penicillin culture," and thrust a tiny round glass jar into her hand.

Major André

General Arnold

THE DRAMA BEGINS as classical tragedy. The scene: the American colonies. The year: 1779. The protagonist: a brave Patriot general, not yet forty. Benedict Arnold has saved his country more than once from military defeat. But there is backstabbing in the ranks: jealous men malign his name; and Congress is ungrateful. He could retire, but he is not a retiring man. He craves action. He wishes—despite a shattered leg (memento of his victory at Saratoga), despite marriage to a beautiful Loyalist half his age—to return to battle. But he sees the revolution usurped by radical ideologues and, disenchanted, he considers his options.

Enter young John André. Handsome but unprincipled, he looted Benjamin Franklin's home of rare books and scientific apparatus when the British evacuated Philadelphia. He sketches, writes poetry, and composes flattering toasts at his general's dinner table. Now chief of the British secret service in occupied New York, he seizes at Arnold's first feeler toward defection.

Tragedy gives way to mystery thriller, complete with code names and clandestine correspondence in invisible ink. For a price the general, by then in command of the strategic forts at West Point, will deliver—West Point! But how, when, at what price? He and André must talk.

The next act is broad comedy. Urgent messages go undelivered, causing the conspirators to seek each other in places where they are not. Country bumpkins hired to row André upriver declare themselves too tired. Still, the meeting at last takes place, in the wee hours of September 22, 1780, on the Hudson River's west bank. The men cannot see each other in the dark, but the parley goes well. At dawn André discovers that he is behind American lines. The next day he is captured, out of uniform, with the plans for West Point in his stocking, and is arrested as a spy.

The end is tragic, but lacks the catharsis of retribution. Arnold escapes and cannot be hanged for his treason. André stands tall, ties a handkerchief over his eyes, and takes the fall for them both.

Ludwig Wittgenstein

Bertrand Russell

IT WAS OCTOBER 1911, volume one of *Principia mathematica* was newly
out, and Bertrand Russell, fellow of Trinity College, Cambridge, was
having his tea when a young man suddenly appeared. He introduced
himself as "Loot'vig Vit'gun-shteyn." Russell replied in German, but the
young man would have none of that. He had studied engineering, he said in
English, but preferred the philosophy of mathematics, and had come to Cambridge expressly to hear Russell on mathematical logic.

Which he did that very day, and throughout the term. He dominated discussions and then followed Russell back to his rooms to press his case, often
far into the night. "He thinks nothing empirical is knowable," Russell com-
plained when the Austrian refused to admit, for example, that there was not a
rhinoceros in the lecture room, even after Russell had checked under all the
tables and chairs. But as Wittgenstein's abilities became more apparent, Russell began to view him as his natural heir in mathematical logic—"*the* young
man one hopes for."

He was—and wasn't. Wittgenstein's intense Teutonic seriousness collided
with Russell's mordant wit. When the war came, Wittgenstein enlisted in the
Austrian army, ignoring the fact that his friends were on the other side. "The
last few days I have thought often of Russell," he wrote from the front. "Does
he still think of me?" But lonely nights on watch could be productive, and during a lull in the fighting he put the *Tractatus* on paper. He finished it just before
his capture by the Italians.

The war changed Wittgenstein. A logical mysticism pervaded his thinking
and seeped into the *Tractatus*, as in its concluding line: "Whereof one cannot
speak, thereof one must be silent." Russell did not much like the *Tractatus*,
which cast doubt on some of his own work. But others did. It became a small
classic, and Wittgenstein returned to Cambridge a legendary figure. He
looked askance at Russell, now a socialist, atheist, and advocate of free love,
writing popular books for a living. Russell's role as mentor was over.

Joan Crawford
Bette Davis

AFTER A YEAR IN HOLLYWOOD playing teary-eyed ingenues in dull movies, Bette Davis is ready to throw in the Kleenex and head back to Broadway. Her bags are packed when Warner Bros. surprises her with a contract and transforms her into a platinum blonde. Film exhibitors take note and in 1932 vote her a "Star of Tomorrow." At the awards banquet the diminutive Davis steps up to the radio microphones and is about to gush her thanks over the airwaves when loud shrieks are heard, followed by the glittering entrance of Joan Crawford and her husband, Douglas Fairbanks, Jr. The radio crew and photographers zoom to the divine couple, leaving Davis stranded, forgotten—and fuming.

Fade to 1935. Davis, too, is now a star. Crawford, her marriage to Fairbanks and her affair with Clark Gable both over, eyes her new leading man, Franchot Tone. Just as their romance heats up, Tone is sent over to Warners to costar in *Dangerous* with Davis. She's married, but falls for Tone anyway. She demands that their scenes together be expanded, which entails more private meetings. Davis is sure she can win the upper-class Phi Beta Kappa from the shallow movie queen. She is wrong. When shooting ends, Crawford and Tone marry. Davis's consolation is her first Oscar.

Cut to 1942. The war is on. Crawford will soon disband her fan club for the duration. Davis wonders whether she should continue acting. "But then I felt that's what the enemy wanted—to destroy and paralyze America. So I decided to keep on working." By 1945 she is the highest-paid woman in America, but soon thereafter the tide turns. Crawford, now at Warners, wins an Oscar for *Mildred Pierce* and replaces Davis as the studio's big money-maker.

The years slip away but the grudges don't. In 1962 both are fifty-four, washed up in Hollywood, and the survivors of four marriages apiece when, in desperation, they sign to costar in *What Ever Happened to Baby Jane?* Bette plays Joan's sister, who, jealous of her sibling's success, schemes to kill her. You could hardly call it a stretch.

Joseph Stalin

Winston Churchill

HERE WAS CHURCHILL, staunch anti-Bolshevist—the man who in 1919 had spearheaded Allied military intervention against the Red army—flying off to Moscow to confer with that commissar of commissars Joseph Stalin. The irony was not lost on either man. But by August 1942, Russia had been under heavy German attack for fourteen months, and the prime minister thought it politic to inform the Soviet marshal personally that his allies were not ready for a second front in Europe that year. Stalin would not be pleased.

State Villa No. 7, where Churchill was taken upon arrival, was a luxurious country house with a more modern bathroom than the one at Chequers, and goldfish in the garden like those at Chartwell. The Soviet leader received Churchill at the Kremlin that evening and, as expected, did not like his news. Stalin exuded displeasure. A man not prepared to take risks could not win a war, he grumbled. Troops must be blooded in battle. Churchill kept his cool. He forbore mention of his host's not-so-distant nonaggression pact with their now shared enemy, and then placated him by divulging plans for Operation Torch, against German forces in North Africa.

Discord continued, but on the last evening, when Churchill came to say good-bye, Stalin softened. He suggested drinks at his own house, which was reached by many twists and turns within the Kremlin. His daughter—a handsome redhead, Churchill observed—laid the table while her father uncorked various bottles. The hour that Churchill had planned for extended to seven. Talk and wine flowed freely, and in a moment of rare intimacy Stalin admitted that even the stresses of war did not compare with the terrible struggle to force the collective-farm policy on the peasantry. Millions of kulaks had been, well, eliminated. The historian Churchill thought of Burke's dictum "If I cannot have reform without injustice, I will not have reform," but the politician Churchill concluded that with the war requiring unity, it was best not to moralize aloud.

George Gordon Byron
Percy Bysshe Shelley

I N THE EARLY SPRING of 1816 two English parties crossed the Channel and headed for Geneva. Lord Byron, barred from France for his radical politics, routed his carriage across Belgium and down the Rhine. Shelley's views were equally subversive but less well known; he traveled via Paris by hired vehicle with Mary Wollstonecraft Godwin, their baby, William, and Mary's stepsister, Claire Clairmont. Both poets were running from wives and domesticity, and Byron from bailiffs and scandal (his adored half sister, Augusta, was expecting) as well. Byron was twenty-eight, Shelley twenty-three.

Shelley's Geneva venture was masterminded by Claire in her pursuit of Byron. In London she had introduced him to Shelley's poems, and Byron had greatly admired *Queen Mab.* So when, one morning after his arrival, he returned from a row on the lake and spotted the Shelley party walking along the *plage,* Byron plunged into the shallow water and splashed toward his fellow poet. It was a Childe Harold kind of gesture. Would Shelley dine with him—alone? He would.

The evening was relaxed. Byron delighted in Shelley's candid narration of his unorthodox career. In the ensuing months the two households rented neighboring dwellings, and breakfasted, walked, and boated together. At night, in the drawing room of the Villa Diodati, they talked of macabre experiments and ghostly sensations. Mary had a nightmare about a poor student who constructed a hideous being that came to life. Claire got pregnant. Byron and Shelley embarked on a weeklong sail that climaxed during a squall when the rudder broke and waves spilled into the boat. Byron took off his coat, Shelley followed, and both sat mute with arms crossed, waiting. Shelley could not swim. Aware that Byron knew it, he was consumed with humiliation that this man, who like Leander had crossed the Hellespont, might feel compelled to save him. The danger passed. Six years later, when off the coast of Italy another squall blew in, Byron was not there.

Berthe Morisot

Edouard Manet

O N DAYS SET ASIDE for copying, the galleries at the Louvre were a sea of easels, professional copyists vying for space with students. Berthe Morisot first went there, chaperoned by her mother, at age sixteen. A descendant of Fragonard and a pupil of Corot, she had by twenty-seven spurned marriage for a life devoted to art. That was the year—1868—that fellow painter Henri Fantin Latour brought Edouard Manet to the Louvre to be introduced.

Morisot knew Manet by reputation—everyone did. His *Déjeuner sur l'herbe* had been the scandal of the Salon des Refusés in 1863, and his *Olympia* was almost hooted off the wall two years later. His family came from the *haute bourgeoisie*, like hers; he was handsome, witty, nine years her senior, and married—not that that concerned her, of course. On the day of the meeting she set up her canvas in the Grande Galerie and selected a delicious Rubens nymph to copy. Others, too, could draw a nude.

The introduction accomplished, Manet was intrigued by the dark-eyed beauty and asked her to sit for him. She found posing a novel experience: Manet strolled about the studio and conversed charmingly as he worked. Morisot sat for twelve paintings, always clothed, always chaperoned; her eyes gaze broodingly, or invitingly, out from the frames. One can only guess at feelings unexpressed—or at how Madame Manet, a stolid Dutch lady, might have viewed it. "He has made a portrait of his wife," Berthe's mother noted. "I think it was about time."

But the artist Morisot also challenged Manet; she curbed his obsession with style and urged him to paint outdoors. Her work, in turn, reflected his. As her self-confidence increased, however, so did her originality and artistic ambition. A distancing began. Degas wooed Morisot into the first Impressionist exhibition; Manet declined. A bond was broken. Morisot's engagement to Edouard's brother Eugène followed. Manet painted one last portrait of her: a gold band is prominent on her ring finger, and her eyes have lost their mystery.

Paul Robeson
Peggy Ashcroft

FOR A BLACK MAN, the question of playing Othello on stage in 1930 was a thorny one, even in England. It had been suggested to Paul Robeson by Mrs. Patrick Campbell eight years before, and at twenty-four he had been flattered and had gone right out to buy a copy of Shakespeare's plays. But the dark Moor's wife is young, beautiful, and *white*—ay, there's the rub—and Othello's skin color had always been a matter of makeup. Now the part was offered him, and he accepted, although there was the risk the London audience that had loved the gentle giant in *Show Boat*, with his marvelous basso "Ol' Man River," would be appalled.

One inducement for Robeson was the chance to select his own Desdemona, and that, at least, proved easy. On a night out at the theater, he saw her onstage—"Miss Peggy Ashcroft," the program read—only twenty-two, but already a presence. He asked her to audition—a daunting prospect to one who, along with her contemporaries, admired him enormously. "I can't sing in tune," she later reported, "and I had to perform the Willow Song in front of Paul Robeson."

Rehearsals began, and the race issue surfaced at once. It wasn't Ashcroft's problem; her stance was Desdemona's own. But the press's prurient interest in public reaction to a black man's embracing a white woman made Robeson tense. "That girl couldn't get near to me," he said later. "I was backin' away from her all the time. I was like a plantation hand in the parlor, that clumsy."

Opening night arrived. Ashcroft got rave reviews, and Robeson twenty curtain calls, but his notices were mixed. He was too genteel, critics said—afraid of losing himself. Indeed, he may have been. His father had begun life as a slave, and it was the actor's ordeal as a black man in a white world that dominated offstage conversation. Ashcroft was all sympathy; she was also powerfully attracted. Later she admitted, without specifics, that "what happened between Paul and myself" was "possibly inevitable." Although both were married, she made no apology for falling in love. Shakespeare would have understood. "She loved me for the dangers I had passed," Othello says, "and I loved her that she did pity them."

Algernon Swinburne
Victor Hugo

SWINBURNE WAS A slight, carroty-topped Eton schoolboy when he began seriously reading Hugo. During holidays he would roam the beach of the Isle of Wight, declaiming Hugolian verse across the waves. On the other side was France, from which his hero had been banished for advocating the republican cause—with himself as its leader—in opposition to Louis-Napoleon. The young English aristocrat was himself a fervent republican. Hugo was fifty, Swinburne fifteen.

Life brought disillusionment to Swinburne, but the master's example never failed him. It was as if he sought to out-Romantic Hugo, in poetry, drama, fiction, life itself. Hugo and the sea—these were the constants in his often erratic existence. One September, Swinburne was visiting a friend on the Normandy coast, and while bathing was carried far out to sea by a treacherous current. Rescued by a fishing boat and wrapped in sailcloth, he was a fantastic apparition, his red hair dripping seawater down his long pale neck as he intoned Hugo's poems to a bemused crew all the way back to shore.

The tale spread; perhaps it was then that Hugo first learned of his disciple. A meeting in Guernsey, site of the rebel poet's exile, never materialized. Then the Second Empire fell. In November 1882, Swinburne, his fiery head dulled with time, was invited to Paris by a white-bearded Hugo for the anniversary celebration of his play *Le Roi s'amuse*. Both men had grown quite deaf. Hugo gave a dinner party; much as he tried, Swinburne understood not a word of the toast in his honor. When he, in turn, lifted his glass to his host and then dashed it to the ground in extravagant homage, Hugo thought only of the broken goblet. A bond had nonetheless been forged. Later, at the theater, neither man could hear the actors, but both already knew the dialogue anyway. "*Etes-vous content?*" Hugo asked in a moment of rare simplicity, and Swinburne replied from his heart that yes, he was.

Lotte Lenya

Kurt Weill

IN THE FREEWHEELING BERLIN of the 1920s, the unconventional was the norm, the bizarre commonplace. There, a solemn, bespectacled cantor's son might very well be attracted by a Viennese Catholic of lower-class parentage and dubious past. A serious young composer/intellectual might even meet and marry—twice—a redheaded, husky-voiced café dancer.

Lenya always made light of their initial contact: she was on stage auditioning; Weill was playing the piano in the pit; she heard his voice but never saw him. Their meeting in the summer of 1924 was another matter. With postwar inflation running high, a hungry Lenya gratefully accepted an invitation from the playwright Georg Kaiser to live with his family at their villa outside Berlin. One Sunday, Weill, who was working with Kaiser on an opera, came out by train. He was told to get off at the station by the lake, and Lenya was sent across to collect him. Of course she would recognize him, Kaiser said, all composers looked alike, and indeed, there he was—thick glasses, receding hairline, typical round musician's hat. Later she would remember the sun on the waves, and how he kept staring at her as she rowed. Lenya was not beautiful, but she was vibrant and interesting, and underneath his mocking facade Weill was a romantic. Before the opera was staged, they married.

They were faithful to each other—Berlin style. He was her dear "Weillchen." When, in collaboration with Bertolt Brecht, Weill wrote the music for *Mahagonny* and *The Threepenny Opera*, there were parts for Lenya—brassy woman-of-the-streets roles for which her warm but abrasive voice was superb. If she, seeking variety, went off from time to time with a lover, and if he took comfort in a mistress—if they even divorced—well, all that passed. So for them did Berlin, thanks to Hitler. America was the haven, the place where her fame grew with his—which was only fair, since, as Weill once told a friend, "my melodies always come to my inner ear in Lenya's voice."

J. Edgar Hoover
Emma Goldman

I N THE FALL OF 1919, Emma Goldman—veteran crusader for nonviolent anarchism, freedom of speech, and birth control—was summoned to a hearing to consider her deportation from the United States. Thirty-four years earlier the young émigré from the Russian ghetto had sailed past the rising pedestal of the Statue of Liberty. Now she faced her inquisitors, chief among them John Edgar Hoover, the fledgling head of the General Intelligence Division of the Department of Justice. Fueled by the hysteria of the Red Scare, he had masterminded the case against Goldman and her friend Alexander Berkman—"dangerous anarchists," he said—while they were in prison for obstruction of the draft. He saw to it that new warrants awaited them on their release, assembled a fat dossier on Goldman's activities, and with a feel for publicity, reactivated a long-disproved charge that she had been complicit in President William McKinley's assassination.

At the hearing Goldman protested the lack of specific charges against her and denounced the proceedings as "utterly tyrannical." But Hoover was interested only in technicalities. Did she claim citizenship through her ex-husband, who had been denaturalized since their divorce? Goldman refused to answer. But the judge seized upon that issue to rule against her and rescind her citizenship.

The resourceful Hoover located an ancient Army transport: its sailing orders were sealed, but it was known to be Russia-bound. Before dawn on the chilly morning of December 21, Goldman, Berkman, and 247 other equally menacing aliens—many of them underfed and ill clad—gathered in the big, brightly lit waiting room on Ellis Island, from where they were loaded onto the "Soviet Ark." Hoover was there; he had even brought a few congressmen up from Washington to witness his triumph. From the deck of the *Buford*, Goldman glowered at him. She loved America, and would not acknowledge that he had won. But she knew he had.

John Wilkes, Esq.

Dr. Samuel Johnson

D<small>R. JOHNSON ABHORRED</small> John Wilkes as a man of no principle. Wilkes was a member both of the notorious Hell-Fire Club and of Parliament; he was a demagogue, a rake. A stay in the Tower for a near treasonous pamphlet made him a hero as a defender of liberty, but Johnson scorned him as a "patriot" in the eighteenth-century sense—a factious disturber of the government. "Patriotism," Johnson sniffed, "is the last refuge of a scoundrel."

Still, Wilkes was good company and frequented London's best dinner tables. But Edward Dilly, the bookseller, was careful not to invite him with Johnson—until the mischievous Boswell proposed just that. Dilly was horrified, but Boswell promised to arrange it.

Boswell: "Mr. Dilly, Sir, sends his respectful compliments," and would Johnson be so good as to dine at his house Wednesday next? He would. Boswell: "Provided, Sir, I suppose, that the company . . . is agreeable?" What if Mr. Dilly asked some of his patriotic friends—for instance, Jack Wilkes? "What is that to me, Sir?" Johnson said huffily. "As if I could not meet any company whatever, occasionally."

Wednesday (May 15, 1776) came, and at dinner Wilkes seated himself next to Johnson. He was determined to please. "Pray, give me leave, Sir," he said, carving Johnson a juicy slice of veal, and then, "a little of the stuffing—some gravy . . . a squeeze of this orange, or the lemon, perhaps?" Johnson's surly response gradually softened. The names of common acquaintances came up, and Wilkes scoffed at those he knew Johnson to have mocked, but the latter would let no one speak ill of his friends but himself. Of Scotland, however— that was another matter. Boswell had taken him there—a barren place! Johnson and Wilkes began sparring with gibes against Scotland. Poor Boswell, Johnson said, hardly knew real civility for living among savages in Scotland and rakes in London. Wilkes beamed. "Except," he said, "when he is with grave, sober, decent people, like you and me."

Mary McCarthy
Edmund Wilson

ON A SATURDAY MORNING in October 1937, the editors of the fledgling *Partisan Review* gathered in their office near Union Square to meet with Edmund Wilson, whom they were courting for the magazine. Wilson enjoyed a cosmopolitan cachet in the New York intellectual scene which they coveted. One editor, Mary McCarthy, had her own agenda, and came in a slinky black dress and a fox stole, remnants of her Vassar days and particularly out of place at the nearby eatery where they all had lunch. It was unclear why, at age twenty-five, she was so anxious to impress this short, stout, squeaky-voiced forty-two-year-old man who barely spoke to her. But she was. And she did.

Two weeks later Wilson invited her to dinner. Her colleagues on the *Review* were afraid she might disgrace them by not being sufficiently modern in her literary tastes; in a briefing that afternoon, one of them pressed daiquiris upon her to prepare her for what he said would be a "dry" dinner. Instead, it began with several rounds of Manhattans, and although McCarthy later recalled trying to be scintillating, she also passed out.

An unpromising beginning—but all writers imbibed wildly in those days. Wilson was charmed by McCarthy's bright intelligence, her impulsiveness, her wooing of him. "Apparently I liked him much more than I remember," she said later.

Enough to marry him, and then question why for the rest of her life. It was his prose style, she once said; another time, his classical education, or because he was upper-class and Protestant—that quarter of her own heritage which she preferred. Or it was what he could do for her as a writer, and did, pushing her into creativity. Or perhaps (her Catholic side) it was as punishment for having gone to bed with him—marriage as absolution for sin. As in all failed unions, there are the given reasons and the real reasons.

Ingrid Bergman

Howard Hughes

Howard Hughes was used to getting what he wanted, and about 1948 he decided he wanted Ingrid Bergman. His days as a daredevil flyer and independent movie producer were over; his millions would always be there. But a beautiful and talented married woman, a symbol of virtue—that was a challenge.

Cary Grant and Irene Selznick arranged an evening when they were all in New York; it ended with dancing at El Morocco. It was very pleasant and civilized, except that Hughes, in his low, clipped Texas voice, kept complaining that he had no friends. Bergman laughed that one off. He could always go out and look for friends, she said. "Anyway . . . you're not lonely tonight, are you?"

That moment of sympathy proved misguided. The phone calls multiplied, to no avail; the lady was not interested. But when she prepared to return to Hollywood, Hughes saw his chance. He bought up all available tickets on every plane flying to California that day, Bergman recalled, and then offered his services. Their flight had its positive side—Hughes had arranged it so that they would hit the Grand Canyon at dawn, and he gave her a guided tour at rim level. That was marvelous, Bergman said. Thank you. Good-bye.

Hughes got one more chance. He phoned one day to inform Bergman that he had just bought RKO—a present for her. She laughed that one off, too— until she wanted to do *Stromboli* with Roberto Rossellini and could not find backing. This time she called him. He was there in fifteen minutes. No, he didn't want to hear the story, he didn't care about the story. Would she be beautiful in it? Would she wear beautiful clothes? She would be playing a refugee in a displaced-persons camp? Ah, too bad—but okay, he would do it anyway.

Whatever Hughes had hoped for didn't happen. What did was the lovely Ingrid's fall from grace in the eyes of her American public. He wrote to her just after little Robertini was born, but she stashed the letter away unanswered. When she found it twenty-five years later, she was awed by its sweetness.

Willie Mays

Leo Durocher

IT IS A SPRING MORNING in Sanford, Florida, 1951. Leo Durocher—once a shortstop with the brawling St. Louis Cardinals' Gas House Gang, now manager of the New York Giants—has driven over to have a look at a hot prospect named Willie Mays. It is only four years since Jackie Robinson broke the color bar in the major leagues, and at nineteen Mays has advanced from the Birmingham Black Barons of his native Alabama through the B league to Triple A ball. This Minneapolis Millers exhibition game has been arranged just so Durocher can see Mays play. "I've got quite a report on you from Trenton, kid," Leo says. Willie: "What did the report say?" Leo: "It said that your hat keeps flying off."

Mays does run fast. This morning he puts on quite a show—a double his first time up, some stunning catches, a stolen base, a home run that clears not only the left-field fence but the clubhouse and railroad tracks, too. When Durocher leaves in the seventh inning, Mays is crushed. What more can a manager want?

By late spring, with the Giants losing steadily, Mays is looking even more impressive. One day the Millers' manager gets a telephone call—Durocher wants Mays right away. Mays panics. "Call him back," he begs. "Tell him I don't want to go to New York. I'm not ready." "Talk to Leo yourself," the manager says. Willie (in his high, piping voice): "I'm not coming." Leo (growling): "What the hell do you mean you're not coming?" Mays admits he's scared. Suppose he can't hit big-league pitching? Leo: "What are you hitting now?" Willie: "Four seventy-seven." Leo: "Well, do you think you can hit two-fucking-fifty for me?" Mays guesses he can.

That's how it began. Durocher was a pugnacious guy, but he saw that this rookie needed bolstering, so he praised him—"rubbed him," he said. It wasn't hard, because he also loved him. Mays hit homers, stole bases, and chased balls all over center field, and in what became a fabled race, the Giants surged from far behind to seize the pennant.

Edgar Degas
Mary Cassatt

Aftee the Civil War it became the fashion for young American women to go off to Paris to study art. This was no ticket to Bohemia. The aspiring *femme peintre* lived with family friends, was prodigiously chaperoned, and after a year or two returned home.

Mary Cassatt was not of that mold. In Paris she studied, she observed, she painted; she visited Italy to do more of the same. She had no intention of returning to America. In 1872 one of her pictures was accepted by the Salon—an achievement almost unheard-of for a young American of either sex. Two years later Edgar Degas saw her portrait *Ida* there and felt an instant affinity; she, in turn, would press against an art-shop window, admiring his pastels.

By 1877 Cassatt's work had become more and more Impressionist and had been twice rejected by the Salon. It was, Degas thought, time to call. In her studio at the edge of Montmartre, he found himself treading on Turkish carpets, peering at beautifully framed paintings hung against tapestried walls and lit by a great hanging lamp. It was his preferred ambience. Before he left, he invited her to exhibit with the Independents. "Most women paint as though they are trimming hats," Degas said. "Not you."

Thus began a forty-year relationship. At first they were seen everywhere together. Degas produced a series of pastels, drawings, and etchings of Cassatt at the Louvre; viewed usually from behind, slim and elegant, she is absorbed in the art before her. It was a condition he understood, as she understood his perfectionism: when a model could not get the particular gesture he was after, Cassatt would place the desired hat on her own head and pose for him herself. On occasion they quarreled, reconciled, quarreled again—never as lovers, which they were not, always as fierce independents.

Degas was not above making Cassatt the butt of derogatory jokes about women painters. But she had the last word. Late in his life she arranged for their work to hang together in New York to benefit a cause she knew he never would have sanctioned—women's suffrage.

Blaise Pascal

René Descartes

ON A SEPTEMBER MORNING in 1647 (Louis XIV, aged nine, was king), a carriage drew up before the Paris house of the Pascal family, and M. René Descartes got out. He looked like a crafty peasant. In fact, at fifty-one, he was the most prominent mathematician-philosopher of his day. His famed *Discourse* divided French intellectuals into two camps—one either was or was not a "Cartesian."

Blaise Pascal, twenty-four, was not. He had no argument with Descartes's axiom "I think, therefore I am," but he was less certain about the ability of reason to prove (a) the existence of God or (b) the nonexistence of a vacuum in nature. Surely God was felt, not reasoned; and as for the vacuum—he had himself only recently conducted experiments that seemed to verify its existence. He was nonetheless pleased when Descartes asked to meet him, and although Pascal was ill, a visit was arranged.

Also present that morning were Professor Roberval, of the Collège de France, a voluble anti-Cartesian, and Pascal's younger sister Jacqueline. Pascal brought out a calculating machine, his recent invention, and demonstrated its ability to add and subtract. Descartes was impressed. The conversation turned to the vacuum. Pascal described his experiment; Descartes expressed doubt—a polite skirmish that might have ended there, but Roberval had not come for civilities. He injected *his* opinion, and a heated argument ensued. Descartes took his leave.

The next morning, however, he returned—not Descartes the philosopher this time, but Descartes the physician. He sat for three hours by his patient's side, listened to his complaints, examined him, prescribed soups and rest. When Pascal was sick of staying in bed, Descartes said, he would be nearly well. Their views would remain opposed, but it was the supreme rationalist in his role as kindly doctor whom Pascal would later remember, and who may have been in his mind when he observed, "The heart has its reasons which reason knows nothing of."

And Concerning the Authors

ON A SUNDAY MORNING in October 1963, a young New Yorker (male) and a migrant from Kansas City (female) happened to sit across from each other in the circle of attenders at Morningside Friends Meeting on the Columbia University campus. For him Quaker silence was a novel experience. For her it was more familiar; what was new was this tall man opposite with the inscrutable face behind the horn-rims. She found him a serious distraction.

During the social hour that followed, it was, of course, perfectly proper to carry a newcomer a cup of coffee and ask him how long he had been in New York, and what he was doing there. A native? She had never met one before. Illustration? How interesting. No, she was not a student—a writer. Published? Of course: the *Columbia Encyclopedia* just out—a tiny but significant part of it was hers. Yes, she would love to have lunch. Yes, today would be fine.

They went to Rumpelmayer's, a charming restaurant favored by elegant ladies after church. He was wearing a corduroy jacket purchased the day before at a flea market for fifty cents. She thought he probably could not afford the taxi, much less lunch at such an establishment, which was well beyond her own budget. She was not dressed for the occasion either. The waiter ushered them to a dark corner and vanished.

There are worse ways to begin a relationship. It turned out he could afford both the taxi and lunch. On their next date they went to a chess parlor and played chess; she won. Friends, when consulted, said that was the worst thing she could have done, but friends can be wrong. On a rainy spring morning a year and a half later, in that same Quaker Meeting, they were married. *First Encounters* is but one of their progeny.

A Note on the Type

This book was set in a modern adaptation of a type designed by the first
William Caslon (1692–1766). The Caslon face, an artistic, easily read
type, has enjoyed two centuries of ever-increasing popularity in
our own country. It is of interest to note that the first copies
of the Declaration of Independence and the first
paper currency distributed to the citizens
of the newborn nation were
printed in this typeface.

Composed by North Market Street Graphics,
Lancaster, Pennsylvania
Color separations, printing, and binding by
Arnoldo Mondadori Editore S.p.A.,
Verona, Italy
Designed by Anthea Lingeman